The Healing Journey - Part I

Beauty
& THE BRUISED
The Courage To Heal

Soleil Meade

Beauty & The Bruised: The Courage To Heal

Copyright © 2026, by Soleil Meade

ISBN: 979-8-218-91727-2

Published by: I Am Handpicked

Printed in the United States of America

DEDICATION

This book is dedicated to the women who have yet to discover the fullness of their purpose because a part of them is still hurting. Healing is not a journey to be conquered alone; it requires God's grace and a community of support. My prayer is that this book becomes a resting place for your heart and a guide toward the wholeness God has promised you.

ACKNOWLEDGEMENTS

First and foremost, to God: As I often declare regarding ministry, this is not my project—it is Yours. Thank you for using me as a vessel to share the experiences, wisdom, lessons, and strategies You've taught me to help others.

To Mom and Joli: You are my rocks, the ones I can count on for wisdom, love, and support in any situation. To my entire family, thank you for loving me when you knew I needed healing, and even when you didn't know. Your presence and our bond are my fuel.

To Apostle Annette, my spiritual mother and purpose pusher: Thank you for speaking into my future, snatching me out of danger, and equipping me for what's to come. You have been with me through the lowest and highest points of my journey. Thank you for being my Harriet Tubman.

To Ms. Domi: I have always viewed life through a spiritual lens, but the season of walking with you therapeutically matured me to a greater level of understanding. Thank you for helping me address my healing and for assisting me in stepping into who God has called me to be.

To Penda: My scribe coach, my sister —This project has been several years in the making, and you never doubted me. You only encouraged me to finish strong. Thank you for pulling the best out of me. You are truly His scribe coach.

To my friends, mentees, and the I Am Handpicked Community: Thank you for holding space for me, giving me the support to grow and trusting me on your journey.

CONTENTS

Beauty
& THE BRUISED
The Courage To Heal

A WOMAN WHO **DESPERATELY** NEEDS GOD MUST

[*Surrender* TO THE **HEALING JOURNEY**]

IN ORDER TO REDISCOVER HERSELF & **PARTNER WITH HIM** WHOLEHEARTEDLY.

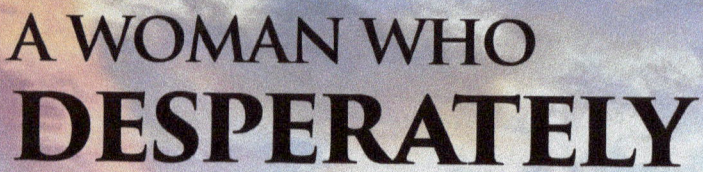

INTRODUCTION

You owe yourself the best version of you: the version that is a surrendered, yet beautiful work of art in progress that God has plans to showcase to the world. He wants to present that version to those who mean the world to you. So, buckle up and get ready for your journey through healing, purpose, and kingdom identity.

Healing requires patience, accountability, vulnerability, and most importantly God. To heal is to rediscover yourself after grasping onto your identity by just a thread. It is courage to face your faults, mistakes, and poor decisions and choose to learn from them. It's the choice to forgive any and everyone who has wronged you and most importantly yourself.

To heal is to believe you are worthy of a second chance in spite of what you've done. It is hitting rock bottom and realizing you were never meant to be there. It is every single action you take to move you from the deep dark place, to the phase of denial, to the functioning yet processing place, and ultimately to your place of freedom, because there are levels to this! Each of us has a healing journey that may have varying requirements, but I can guarantee you two things:

1. You are not alone, someone else can understand the pain you can't put into words. Someone has walked a similar road as you.

2. You cannot heal without a commitment to yourself. God wants to heal you. He needs you to want it and be ready for the journey no matter what you may discover along the path. (Matthew 9:22)

Commitment To Healing

Author's Dedication : My Call To Healing

The moment I realized I had to stop fighting my past and truly heal was when it everything changed. I came face-to-face with my own blind spots. Those hidden areas made me question my character: How can I truly please God, live for Him, and lead others to Him when I have these dark areas in my life? Self-deception minimized my failing heart condition as "small flaws" that weren't visible enough to influence the work I did for Christ. That was a lie! While the flaws seemed small and unnoticeable to others, they were gaping, fleshy wounds in my heart needing immediate attention.

In that critical moment of clarity, my act of surrender was singular: I surrendered who I thought I was to God and chose to release any desire for attention, approval, or applause, allowing God to be my only source of identity. I experienced a raw and real mindset and heart posture shift, loaded with transparency, that led me to another chance at REAL freedom in Him.

On my journey, God has led me from brokenness to identity and intimacy with Him, and that is the same journey I am called to bring to you. This book is founded on the revelation that the Holy Spirit is not just our Comforter but a Dismantler, breaking down trauma and toxic mindsets so He can guide us in Truth. Through Christ's redemption and the Holy Spirit's power, we can experience complete renewal and wholeness. I was created for use by Him to serve as a living witness—a reflection of the healing I've received and that His word promises—to guide others to their own freedom in Him.

My promise to you is unwavering:
You can receive the same transformative healing and grace I have found.

Author's Prayer and Blessing

My prayer is that God will continue to use me to minister healing to His daughters while living a life that reflects the freedom I received and teach. I pray that you will be COMPLETELY Free, postured to relinquish control over every area of your life, and empowered to spread the Good News, including your testimony. May we heal together through the love of God our Father, the redemption of Christ, and the power of the Holy Spirit. Amen

The greatest gift that comes from this surrender is FREEDOM.

It's easy to applaud and celebrate the good things in life, but often difficult to find those who will weather the challenges and ever-evolving script of life.

It is truly an honor to be equipped by God to walk through both celebratory and critical moments of your journey with you.
May God richly bless you for wanting more of Him!

Signed in Faith

Soleil Meade

Your Personal Commitment To Healing

This is your moment to sign your covenant and dedicate your journey to the only one who can make it complete. As you write your name, you commit to shedding every past hindrance and embracing the healed future God has prepared for you.

I, _____, stand before God today, choosing freedom over my past.

I dedicate myself to pursuing the healed woman God sees me as. I relinquish all control over my past, present, and future and surrender every restricted and prohibited area of my heart. I will be transparent with my process and embrace the Holy Spirit as my Comforter and Dismantler.

I am letting go of all unhealed wounds, past traumas, and poor heart and mind postures. I commit to simply allowing Christ to be the Leader of this process, knowing as I surrender, He will do the work that leads to my freedom . I receive a greater measure of faith today to complete this journey of healing and wholeness.

Embracing The Journey

A journey is the path one travels to reach a desired destination. Some journeys are short term, where the path gets you from point A to point B, then it's complete. Some journeys are more complex where the desired destination is clear, but the steps to complete the journey are unexpected and sometimes unknown.

Complex journeys tend to remove the essence of time from our control although we may still try to control it, we quickly learn that our impatience has made the journey even more complex. A prime example is the beloved Israelites who took 40 years to complete a journey (Numbers 32:13) that should have taken 11 days (Deuteronomy 1:2), literally something that could have been accomplished within a little over a week took them 4 decades.

Some of us are on prolonged journeys because we won't surrender to God and allow Him to heal, reshape, and restore us. Some journeys are pleasant to experience while others are challenging, sometimes traumatic. We are all on a journey, but the power comes when we acknowledge our journey should shift us from just living to survive to living to thrive. There are so many factors to influence the path one takes.

How To Take The Journey

Over ten years ago one of my best friends, Kellie Ugwu, called me and shared a dream she had about me. She said she saw me taking people by the hand and leading them from the Kingdom of darkness into the Kingdom of Light. I would complete a trip then go back for more people just like Harriet Tubman did on the Underground Railroad. I was young in my walk with Christ at the time, on fire for God, but I had no clue exactly what He had in store for me. I received the Word and began to study Harriet Tubman.

Harriet Tubman was also known as Moses and the conductor of the Underground Railroad because how Moses led the Israelites out of captivity in Egypt, she led many slaves up North to freedom. She is quoted as saying:

"I was the conductor of the Underground Railroad for eight years, and I can say what most conductors can't say; I never ran my train off the track and I never lost a passenger."

I know it is only God who has tasked me to walk with you. Over years of ministry and experience, I've learned that a special kind of grace is required to walk WITH someone. It was said that a journey through the Underground Railroad could be anywhere from 5 days to 3 weeks of moving in the night on land and at times through water from safe house to safe house, while evading slave catchers and enduring the elements on the journey to freedom. She hand delivered each passenger across the threshold of freedom. In life I've found myself misunderstood at times because of my commitment to see someone through their journey. Not just dropping information or encouragement and leaving but being WITH you until you reach breakthrough and freedom in Christ.

I'm fully aware that I cannot do this work for you. There's no way Harriet could have freed as many as she did carrying them on her back or dragging them along. She had to have passengers who were ready to risk it all for freedom. Willing to do the work, teachable, alert, and committed to the journey. She needed passengers to trust her even when she had to pivot or shift directions. She needed passengers that listened to her voice, gestures, and commands as she led them step by step. It took three to complete the journey to freedom – a God ordained guide, a courageous faith filled soul ready to work for freedom, and God who is the author and finisher of our faith.

"I freed a thousand slaves. I could have freed a thousand more if only they knew they were slaves."
~Harriet Tubman

I've always held that prophesy about being like Harriet Tubman close to me because it reminded me that God called and equipped me for this. Others may not understand it or call it crazy, I'm sure they called Harriet and Moses crazy too, but that's what He purposed them to do. To guide a people who are trapped, oppressed and in darkness into freedom and light through the power of God.

ALL ABOARD the healing journey! Let's work together with Him to gain freedom and healing!!!

This book comes from my hard lessons, faith, perseverance, patience and so much more that I had to go through and conquer before I could lead you through it. Let me help you prepare your bag for the journey with our first worksheet.

ALL ABOARD

What's In Your Bag?

JOURNEY PREPARATION WORKSHEET

Your healing journey is unique, and just like any significant journey, preparation is key. What tools, resources, and support will you pack to ensure you're equipped for the path ahead? Let's start packing for your healing journey. Choose from the packing list and search yourself for what you personally need to thrive.

Instructions:

1. Review the categories below.

2. From the "Packing List" bank, select the items that resonate with you as necessary for your healing journey.

3. Add any additional items that come to mind.

4. Reflect on why each item is essential for you.

PACKING LIST

Bible

Personal Journal

Peaceful/Safe Space

Spiritual Mentor

Accountability Partner

Self Care

Community/ Friends

Kleenex

Prayer

Fasting

Emotional Check-Ins

Commitment to God

Therapist

Worship Music

Healing Scriptures

Positive Self-Talk

Goals/Vision

Family Support

Dedicated Attention

Forgiveness

Now that you've completed this worksheet, how will you prepare? Consider creating a safe space or arranging for support like childcare. Journal your plan here.

_____

_____

_____

I invite you to take this Healing Journey with me. There is great purpose inside of YOU that isn't connected to what happened to you, who people say you are or what you do for anyone else. God wants you to experience honor, love, respect, dignity, confidence, grace, and character that is exclusively curated for you. Take this healing journey for yourself, but remember, you are not alone.

From 2020-2022 I hosted healing cohorts to test the material in this book. A resounding message was clear to me when some of the participants mentioned how comforting it was to know that they were not alone and others were having similar experiences. Those thoughts of "No one understands," began to slowly lose the bass in its voice.

Here is my letter to healing, so you can see my personal journey before you embark on your own:

Dear Healing

Thank you for being a REAL friend. I emphasize REAL because some people just want to be around to experience the fun and good parts of you, but a REAL friend is right there with you in the darkest times. Initially when you came around I was leary of you. Like why would you come all close to me to remind me of my past, start talking to me about things I buried deep in hopes they wouldn't surface. I'll never forget the internal anguish I felt when you had me sit in the fact that due to my decision making (poor at that time), I was not a mother... ON MOTHER'S DAY.

When I tell you that thing stung and hit deep!!! I remember after I had sobbed and cried until my eyes were puffy, I felt this release. A REAL friend will give you a sense of relief in the most unbearable times. Something in me couldn't just move on from the emotion I felt — I knew I needed to sit in it. It was in that moment you helped me see that those poor decisions caused condemnation, guilt, distrust, and so many other nasty things in me, were more harmful buried inside of me. I felt worthy to desire something more for myself and no longer carry that pain deep inside. You helped me to feel free!

You assured me that there was better for me and I was not being punished for my decisions. We had many moments like this friend and every time, it was this process of "Sheesh! You didn't have to hit me so hard with the truth", then these moments of realizing that facing the hard truth was making me a better person, it was redeeming my self worth, giving me clarity, and even bettering my relationships.

You are truly a good friend. You are accountability but comfort. You are tears but both good and bad tears. You are comfort when I feel lost, confused, and unworthy. You are peace when life is chaotic. You are hope when I felt hopeless. You are REAL when I chose to be fake and wear masks. You are the light at the end of the tunnel when I couldn't see the light at all. You have consistently been what I need more than what I wanted and every time you proved yourself right. Healing, you are none other than the love and power of God.

Like the Golden Girls theme song, thank you for being a friend, travel down the road and back again. Your heart is true, you're a pal and a confidant. Thank you Healing for being the REAL friend I didn't know I need but couldn't live without.

love Soleil

Help Me Heal
WORKSHEET

Use this worksheet to dissect and understand your healing process.
May the Lord honor, bless, and cleanse you fully as you yield to the process.

Step 1- Heart Check
What do I need to heal from?

_____
_____
_____
_____
_____

Step 2- Mind Shift
What is within me to overcome this?

_____
_____
_____
_____
_____

Step 3- Root Reveal
What barriers/triggers are in my way?

_____
_____
_____
_____

Step 4- Fight Strategy
What ways do I fight these barriers?

_____
_____
_____
_____

While sharing our experience with others can be liberating, I want to remind you that our Lord and Savior knows a lot about healing. Not only is He our Healer, but Jesus had to go on his own healing journey to offer salvation and redemption to us.

As you reviewed the areas you need to heal in the Help Me Heal Worksheet, I hope you are reminded of what Jesus went through, including being traumatized, violated, and wounded deeply; the very same bruises and trauma you have had to endure.

Resting Places

Look for spaces throughout the book that are designed to help you rest and reflect. I call them, Permission to Pause. In these resting spaces, there are questions for you to answer to help you reflect on your journey. Here is your first rest stop and you have Permission to Pause along with a video from your conductor.

HELP ME HEAL

PERMISSION TO PAUSE

In what ways are you desperate for God?

_____

_____

_____

_____

_____

_____

_____

_____

_____

_____

What do you need to surrender to Him?

_____

_____

_____

_____

_____

_____

_____

_____

_____

_____

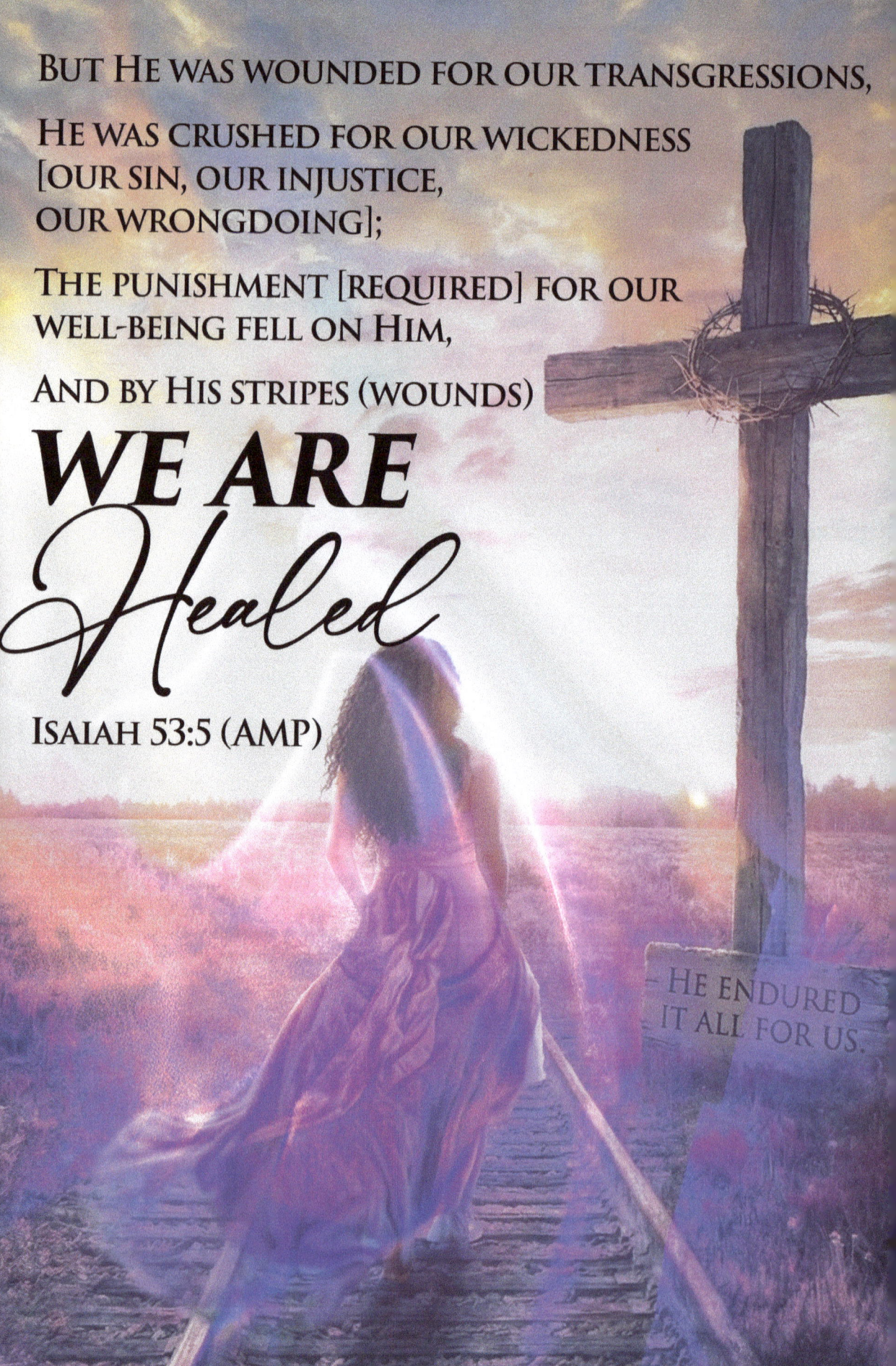

BUT He was wounded for our transgressions,

He was crushed for our wickedness
[OUR SIN, OUR INJUSTICE,
OUR WRONGDOING];

The punishment [required] for our
well-being fell on Him,

And by His stripes (wounds)

WE ARE
Healed

ISAIAH 53:5 (AMP)

HE ENDURED
IT ALL FOR US.

1

SURRENDER AND SILENCE THE PAST

Let's travel down memory lane and revisit a childhood memory that I treasure. Life was easy, full of happy songs, and fairytale stories I only wished someday could be me. (Little did I know…) One of my favorite Disney movies is *Beauty and the Beast*. I loved every song in the movie, and Chip was the cutest little teacup ever. I thought Belle was one of the power Princesses; she was smart, pretty, and unashamed. She didn't want to be put in a box, but wanted to explore life and fill it with people and things that made her feel free to be her (even if it was the sheep she was reading her books to). I thought she was a beautiful princess inside and out!

Belle was so brave to take her dad's place and stay in the castle with the Beast. When I looked at the true meaning of the story, beyond my obsession with Disney Princesses, I see that we are invited into the process it takes for one to transform the ugly parts of themselves but only by experiencing something beautiful – TRUE LOVE. It boasts of the chance to love and be loved again after selfish and unkind choices.

My Mask, His Moment

Some years ago, on my birthday, August 7th, I spent my day making memories. I did things I love with people I treasure. My dinner with family and friends was fun and powerful. I made a statement to them, "I feel like this year is going to be one of the greatest years of my life!"

I felt God shifting things in my life and I was not going to miss out on it. I then proceeded to pass my journal with my fancy rose gold pen around the table to my guests, asking them to write a word of encouragement to me to reflect on throughout the year. Little did I know, I would need those words to anchor me as I navigated through the transitions and challenges that would be later known as my healing journey. A necessary route designed to move me to where God wanted me to be.

I spent the last hours of my birthday reading their messages and praying. The next day I made a post on Facebook, that was aligned with the shift I spoke about the night before. This post didn't go viral, but this led several women to my inbox asking for help and looking for hope!

After sharing with several women about being broken and bruised, and listening to their stories, I knew this was bigger than a Facebook post. God began to show me that Beauty and the Bruised was a healing space for women - affirming their beauty while helping them heal from their bruises. But, how could I help others heal, when I needed healing?

I told them "It's Possible," but that was a BOLD blindfolded, faith move. A week before that birthday, I was still trying to salvage a relationship where I was GHOSTED... left crushed, confused, and bruised. I had never been so vigilant in seeking God about any relationship, there was something about this one I wanted to protect.

I wanted to get myself right and be at my best for him, and for us. I don't know how I was in the space to type that message about loving again; I was nursing multiple bruises. Only a few knew how much I was suffering on my birthday, crying for answers and help, angry for being mistreated, yet somehow beautiful and glowing in my birthday photos (we'll talk about the masks we wear later)!

But God Knew! It was my mask, but He was delivering me a moment of a lifetime. The first two photos are what I posted on my birthday - happiness, joy and celebration. The last photo was the reality of how I felt deep inside captured on camera. You can see the dullness in my eyes in the last photo. The sun can be shining on you but if your mind, heart, and emotions are wrestling with hurt and pain, it will show.

Just like with Beauty and the Beast, I needed to transform the ugly, bruised parts of myself, even if they were caused by someone else, through experiencing a deeper level of healing and true love—from God!

Behind The Mask

WORKSHEET

Use this worksheet to identify the feelings, thoughts, mindsets, you stuff deep down inside hoping your mask will hide it. What situations have you worn a mask and no one knew.? What do you use as a mask? Take some time to reflect and write or draw your reflections in the open space.

Soleil Meade
August 8, 2019 · 🌐

···

It's so difficult to preserve genuine
and pure love in your heart after it's
been broken and bruised ...
but I'm here to tell you
IT'S POSSIBLE!!

How do you relate to this statement?

_____

_____

_____

Can you recall a time when you felt broke, bruised, and unable to
love or trust again?

_____

_____

_____

_____

Do you believe your love can be restored?

_____

_____

_____

The Anatomy Of Bruises

Typically when you break a bone you might get a cast to protect and support it better but when you're bruised you kind of just have to let it heal on its own.

Merriam Webster defines a bruise as: an injury involving rupture of small blood vessels and discoloration without a break in the overlying skin an injury especially to the feelings

And bruising as: to break down by pounding to inflict psychological hurt on

What stood out to me is *"without a breaking in the overlying skin."* Bruising is an outside source causing an inward injury to manifest visibly. Sounds a lot like heartbreak, betrayal, mental and emotional abuse from someone who's supposed to love us. Bruises are painful and ugly. We try to mask them with makeup; even though others can't see it, we feel it. Sometimes we wear certain clothing in attempts to cover our bruises, but the fabric brushing against sensitive skin is torturous. Sometimes the bruises are so bad we isolate ourselves, so we don't have to tell the story of the bruise.

This explains the physical nature of bruises, and directly correlates to the emotional bruises many of us endure.

We bury the story along with all the feelings, hoping its humiliation, pain, disgrace, and hurt never surface. We wear the mask of dressing ourselves up all pretty—makeup done, smile bright, glowing like one of God's best daughters, only to fall apart during the end of the night while staring in your mirror asking God, Who am I? Why is this happening to me? What did I do to deserve this? Emotionally the bruising can make us hard, calloused and full of resentment one day, then soft, sensitive, and pitiful the next.

The good news is research shows that physical bruising typically heals without treatment in about two weeks. But what about bruised hearts, hopes, expectations, and identity? There isn't a general treatment plan because we all heal differently. I invite you on this journey of exploring and conquering the hurts, pains, and bruising in your life, with the intent to help you:

- Know You Are Not Alone.

- Identify the sources of your beauty and bruises.

- Understand Your Healing & Your Purpose Are Essential.

- Relate with a commonality many women share of how continual bruising by others or self can create toxic mindsets and behaviors.

- Understand You Must Divorce Toxic Mindsets & Behaviors.

- Commit to healing by experiencing TRUE LOVE from God, like Beast did.

- Know You Are Seen and Worthy of Love.

   One definition of bruising is "to break down by pounding." When you view it this from the lens of mental and emotional bruising, our soul (mind, will, and emotions) are literally taking a beating— being broken down and pounded on. When you reach this state it is likely the damage is so overwhelming, you begin to become unrecognizable, internally and externally. Those outbursts and intrusive thoughts drown out the sanity and common sense you had. The comments of "You look tired!", or " You always have something going on!" At that point you don't even recognize who you've become.

We began to not feel ourselves as we entertain negative self-talk, replay over and over again those things done against us or the mistakes we've made, sulk in pity, ride the rollercoaster repeatedly until we're sick, isolate from everyone and everything we possibly can, subscribe to depression, and sometimes fall back into old self-serving behaviors that are no good for us. Pain has a way of trying to define you, but pain is not who you are, it's merely what you experiencing in that moment.

Pain doesn't have to last when you allow hope, restoration, forgiveness, love, reconciliation, faith, and all their friends to take over the space. Let the Healer in.

PERMISSION TO PAUSE

It's time to face pain! Take a moment to journal in victory over the pain.
Tell it what it cannot call you any longer, how it won't affect you in its
familiar ways anymore, how your mind will be vs. how it used to be.

_____

_____

_____

_____

In what ways have I allowed pain to define you?

_____

_____

_____

_____

What have people said about you?

_____

_____

_____

_____

What have you believed about yourself that contradicts who you
really are?

_____

_____

_____

_____

Beauty & The Bruised Testimony: 12 Long Years

Let's look at a shining example of this in the Bible of a woman navigating the spectrum of bruised to blessed.

"Then a woman who had suffered from a hemorrhage for twelve years came up behind Him and touched the [tassel] fringe of His outer robe; for she had been saying to herself, "If I only touch His outer robe, I will be healed." But Jesus turning and seeing her said, "Take courage, daughter; your [personal trust and confident] faith [in Me] has made you well." And at once the woman was [completely] healed."

Matthew 9:20-22 AMP

Imagine being on your period or having some issue that has you bleeding for 12 years! Let's sit with her for a minute. We are women so we can empathize to an extent with her pain, discomfort, odor, hormones, emotion, loneliness, hopeless moments, confusion, loss of normalcy (like marrying, having kids) and dejection. Images generally depict her crawling on the dusty ground and pushing through a crowd to get to Jesus. She's being stepped on and walked over, but she's desperate for healing. No one is paying attention to her except Jesus. She has tried everything and see Jesus as her only hope. Her faith ignites her to go after her healing.

The woman with the issue of blood is teaching us the process, posture, and passion associated with healing.

Healing is a Process

Like the woman with the issue of blood, you move from Despair > To Faith > To Healing. We cannot heal if we stay in that dark place. We cannot heal if we return to that dark place. We simply cannot stay where we are! It's imperative to commit to the process… no matter how challenging it becomes.

The woman with the issue of blood was committed to her healing process. She broke the law for her healing, risked being ostracized and outcast from her city, being mocked for being unclean, being trampled on further which likely agitated her pre-existing pain but she didn't give up! I'm sure she fought through multiple scenarios of why she shouldn't push through, recalling the times she had subscribed to the narrative that she was unclean and unworthy, but she fought her way out of those mindsets, divorcing them so she could be free.

Just like her, we cannot abandon the mission which is to achieve healing through the almighty power of Jesus.

Healing Requires Posture Shifts

She was in pain as well as pursuit with postured eyes as she searched through a crowd for that exact garment that belonged to Jesus. Her arms were postured to reach and lunge out to touch Jesus' garment and receive healing. Her meek yet truthful posture shined bright when she had the courage to respond to Jesus after he said, "Who touched me?" (Luke 8:45) Lastly this woman had a posture of trust, confidence, faith, hope for a fresh start when Jesus told her she was healed. Your posture during your process has a significant impact on your outcome, especially the time spent in the process.

Healing Requires A Passion

Most times when we think of passion we think of what we love to do, but let's look at what can happen when we're passionate about what we want or need to happen.

Passion is defined as an intense, driving, or overmastering feeling or conviction, a strong liking or desire for or devotion to some activity, object, or concept.

This woman was passionate about her healing. Too often we're so beat down by the bruising phase we just want to stuff the pain down enough so we can still "function". When you're passionate about your healing you cannot keep the pain in, you won't stop at finding some kind of solution, you'll go to extreme measures to get to your healing.

My prayer is that this story will help you achieve those goals we discussed earlier regarding healing.

- You are not alone.

- Your Healing and Purpose Are Essential.

- You must divorce toxic mindsets and behaviors. Y

- ou Are Seen and Worthy Of Love.

Now that you've acknowledged some of your bruises and have been equipped with knowledge, wisdom, and Biblical examples on how to navigate those bruises, let's prepare to understand the power of healing.

How do you relate to this woman? (Her condition? Her surrender?)

_____

_____

_____

_____

_____

How does her "if I could just" statement similar to yours?

_____

_____

_____

_____

Describe her posture of faith.

_____

_____

_____

_____

YOUR WOUND IS PROBABLY NOT YOUR FAULT, BUT YOUR *Healing* IS YOUR RESPONSIBILITY

- Unknown

Dear Healing

Thank you for lifting the weight of the masks, pain, and secrets that were invisible to the public but suffocated me. I thank God for you Healing, I feel like I can breathe again.

LEAN IN

2

THE POWER OF HEALING

Listen I get it! This is the hard part! This is the part where defensiveness and self-pity starts to rise up. This is also where the security blankets you've used to protect yourself, whether good or bad, want you to just sulk and wrap up in them. I know it's uncomfortable, but I need you to stay in there with me. You have to face the ugly, yet real parts of yourself.

Self-assessment is critical to growth. So as hard as it may be, I need you to assess your current state so you'll know exactly what you need healed from.

Go back and read your commitment statement you created, revisit what you want to be free from and allow that to help you stand ten toes down on this healing journey.

Pain has a way of trying to define you and convince you that you only amount to what happened to you, the trauma you experienced, the strong emotions you feel inside. But the truth is pain was just an experience and God's PURPOSE and plan for you is who you are!

Face the Pain

Healing is a journey; it's uncomfortable, requires patience & commitment, often shows us things in ourselves and others we'd rather not see. Healing develops some of the best parts of our character and testimony. It makes us relatable to others and reminds us thar we're humans in need of a great God.

Merriam-Webster defines healing as the process of making or becoming sound or healthy again. To become sound or healthy again. To alleviate (a person's distress or anguish), correct or put right (an undesirable situation.

We have so much to unpack about healing but one of my favorite parts of this definition is the word "again". If healing is *becoming sound again*, that means there was a time when you were sound. Again is a promise to put you back in your right place and position mentally, physically, emotionally, and spiritually through the power of God. I love the definition Collins dictionary provides: *once more in a previously experienced or encountered place, state, or condition.* So, if you could imagine yourself at a time when you were healed and free, the word again delivers hope that you can return there. The bonus for us is with God we can return and expect exceedingly and abundantly.

Throughout scripture we find the word again used in many ways and formats. In the New Testament, the Greek word for again is *anastasis* which means *"a raising up; A rising from the dead. The resurrection of certain one's history who were restored to life."*

I need you to know that AGAIN is your portion. You will hope again, dream again, love again, trust again, believe again as you continue along your healing journey.

Grab your favorite Bible Study tool or app (I recommend Blue Letter Bible App) and do a search on the word "again."

How many times does it show up in the bible?

_____

_____

_____

In what context is it used?

_____

_____

_____

_____

What is the message "again" speaking to your healing journey?

_____

_____

_____

_____

What scripture containing "Again" stands out to you the most?

_____

_____

_____

_____

The Anatomy Of Healing

Healing is the process of the restoration of health from an unbalanced, diseased, damaged or devitalized organism. (Wikipedia).

Let's look into the anatomy of healing in our bodies. The reference shares it as an unbalanced, diseased, damaged, or unvitalized organism. That organism is you. In order for us to start our healing journey we must acknowledge where we are.

The healing process can be activated when you're able to identify signs and symptoms in you that indicate you are:

- Unbalanced: not in equilibrium; mentally disordered; affected with mental illness; not adjusted so as to make credits equal to debits

- Diseased: affected with or as if with a disease : lacking health or soundness : sickly

- Damaged: loss or harm resulting from injury to person, property, or reputation

- Devitalized: to deprive of life, vigor, or effectiveness

With physical damage or disease suffered by an organism, healing involves the repair of living tissue(s), organs and the biological system as a whole and resumption of (normal) functioning. Medicine includes it as the process by which cells in the body regenerate and repair to reduce the size of a damaged or necrotic (dead) area and replace it with new living tissue.

The replacement can happen in two ways:

1. Regeneration in which the necrotic cells are replaced by new cells that form "like" tissue as was originally there.

2. Repair in which injured tissue is replaced with scar tissue.

Most organs will heal using a mixture of both regeneration and repair. It's also important to note that healing requires repair in multiple areas – physically and scientifically speaking living tissues, organs and the biological system as a whole.

Spiritually you can look at the anatomy of healing to repair your heart, mind, soul and spirit. When you apply this to your healing journey you are positioned to anticipate those bruises and pains you named in the last chapter will be repaired or replaced with new truths regarding your life and purpose.

The beautiful phenomenon of healing is that it doesn't completely disregard the damaged or injured parts of your journey. Regeneration and repair processes use the damaged parts to learn from them and even utilizes the scars they've produced to play a major part of developing something new in you.

So as painful as that hurt was, as much as you'd like to forget it... I want to remind you that God wastes NOTHING!! Even the hurt you endured has purpose when you heal (Romans 8:28).

Let's take a moment to digest what we learned about healing at this next resting place.

PERMISSION TO PAUSE

Do the credits poured into your life equal the debits other's take?

_____

_____

_____

_____

_____

_____

What areas of your life are sick and unhealthy?

_____

_____

_____

_____

What, who, where in life has injured your body, emotions, mind, value, etc.? How does this surface in new relationships, with family, self-worth?

_____

_____

_____

_____

_____

_____

_____

_____

Let's look into some biblical references that translate to formulas that help you to understand how to activate your faith during your healing journey and God's response to our action.

Formula 1

If my people, who are called by my name, will humble themselves and pray and seek my face and turn from their wicked ways, then I will hear from heaven, and I will forgive their sin and will heal their land. 2 Chronicles 7:14

This scripture is encouraging us to activate.

Humble Yourself and Pray- The Hebrew word for humble is *kana*, meaning, to be subdued, brought down, to be low, brought under subjection, to humiliate. This is the time to be wrecked before God and lay it all before Him in prayer. To humiliate means to feel ashamed and foolish from injuring one's dignity and self-respect. The type of atmosphere this humbling will create, is one of repentance, forgiveness, and restoration.

Seek God's Face - Here is where you are earnestly looking for God's face to receive His correction, guidance, direction, love, encouragement and everything else He has to offer. The Hebrew word for seek is *bāqaš* that encourages us to seek not only to find but to secure and demand the face of God. Your seeking is calling God to action in your life.

Turn from your wicked ways- The expectation here is to continue in the spirit of repentance which means to turn away from sin or in the case of our healing journey anything you identified you need to heal from.

In response to our activation, God will do the following:

- Hear from heaven,

- Forgive their sins,

- Heal their land.

Here we're dealing with an if/then statement which is contingent on the if. So if you activate, God will move on your behalf. He will consult with heaven for you, forgive the heavy burdens you've been carrying and deliver healing to you. This is His promise! Do your part.

Formula 2

Therefore, confess your sins to one another [your false steps, your offenses], and pray for one another, that you may be healed and restored. The heartfelt and persistent prayer of a righteous man (believer) can accomplish much [when put into action and made effective by God—it is dynamic and can have tremendous power]. James 5:16 AMP

This scripture encourages us to activate and magnify the power of unity:.

Confess Your Sins To One Another. Too often we try to keep our issues between "me & God" but here we are being charged to confess our sins to one another. This looks like you finding your accountability partner, someone you can trust with your truth and gaining power over that truth by sharing it. The enemy knows secrets are like a poison to us, so he wants us to hold that toxicity. The Hebrew word for confess is *exomologeō* which means to confess, profess, and acknowledge openly and joyfully. Remember that if joy is paired with your confession, then you're likely in a place where you're expecting the confession to give you freedom.

Pray for One Another. You can't confess your sins without any follow up action. It's important that you and your accountability partner seal that confession with repentance and decrees of faith, hope, and love. The confession has presented an understanding of the weight, intensity, and details of the sin so now that we know it well, we are equipped to pray against any spirit, mindset or emotion at work, speak well over their purpose, direction, healing, and more.

In response to our activation, God will heal and restore.

A Healed Version Of You

Begin to envision a healed version of you. I understand this may be challenging but YOU CAN DO IT! Scan the code for a message of encouragement on how I see you healed. On the next page you'll find my example of speaking to the healed version of me.

I SEE YOU HEALED!

TO THE VERSION OF ME WHO
SURVIVED

Hey Sunshine,

I need you to know that you are loved. There is nothing wrong with you, and there is nothing more you can do—outside of being the extraordinary human God made you to be—to cause people to love, like, or accept you. You don't realize this, but your light is like a mirror to people. Sometimes they run from you because the sincerity and purity of your love and concern holds a mirror to them, causing them to see the broken parts in them that resist true love and care.

I need you to know that your love is special, and not everyone can handle the depths, complexities, yet ease with which you're able to give it. I'm really sorry you went through so many friendships and relationships that made you question how God built you to love and care for others. Despite how they treated and left you, they still needed your love and light in their lives. I know it left you broken, feeling inadequate, and unworthy of love and relationship in so many ways. But you are stronger than you think and truly a sucker for a redemption story. I am so glad you finally embraced that God's love is enough for you and built your relationship with Him. It's one of the best decisions you've made. (I just wish we would have done it sooner, but it's all good because God doesn't waste anything, girl!)

God has turned everything you've been through into something He can use—to grow you, to mature you, to prepare you to minister to others, and to make you relatable and REAL to those He's assigned to you. Thank you for not cracking, breaking, or giving up. Thank you for not falling in too deep with depression. Thank you for having enough wisdom to say "enough is enough," even if it took a little while. Thank you for never accepting failure as a word to describe you. Because you didn't allow these attempts to overtake you, we are healing today!

We made it to a pretty great version of us, and there's so much more to come. I love you, girl!! Let's light up the world (John 15:16).

Healed Soleil

Dear Healing

You look good on me girl!!
Thank you for seeing the
healed version of me,
even in my ugly stage!

3

HEALING FOR RELATIONSHIPS

Relationships and connections are the heartbeat of our existence. God created the heavens, and the Earth, and all the beauty within. When He created Adam, God said in Gen 2:18 "It is not good that the man should be alone, I will make him a help meet." Even from the beginning of time, we find that relationships are vital to our existence. I desire to help you create healthier and solid relationships in life. I have experienced some of the most amazing relationships along with quite a few shattering ones in my lifetime.

Relationship & Intimacy

The Oxford dictionary defines relationship as:
the way in which two or more concepts, objects, or people are connected, or the state of being connected; the way in which two or more people or groups regard and behave toward each other.

Oxford defines intimacy as:
a close familiarity or friendship; closeness, closeness of observation or knowledge of a subject; a private, cozy atmosphere

I would love to expand your mindset on relationships and intimacy. When looking at the standard definitions above, you can distinctly see that the premise of relationships is connection while intimacy is closeness and privacy. It appears that intimacy requires a deeper level of knowing and understanding someone, because you can be connected to someone through various controlled and uncontrollable factors but still not close or familiar with them. Yet with intimacy there is clear intention and desire for attachment and connection. I personally believe in striving for intimacy in every relationship in my life and viewing intimacy beyond the bedroom. We so often equate intimacy solely with sex that we miss out on the most fulfilling opportunities to create intimate moments in everyday life—Intimacy with God, intimacy with your family & loved ones, intimacy with your vision/goals, etc.

My definition of intimacy is :
engaging/knowing someone or something thoroughly, to the deepest parts, personal, private, exclusive attention, devotion of time, mental, emotional and physical space.

My sister in Christ, Terina J. Hicks said, "Into Me See". Intimacy looks beyond the surface but into the deep parts of who you are, your behavior, how you think, speak, and function. Intimacy says "I love you even though you haven't quite become who you're destined to be. It just brings me joy watching you BECOME."

INTIMACY IS
KNOWING
SOMEONE OR SOMETHING THOROUGHLY,
TO THE DEEPEST PARTS

Personal, Private, Exclusive Attention, Devotion Of Time, Mental, Emotional and Physical Space

I've learned that once your standard is set for how you plan to show up, it's more your responsibility than anyone else's to ensure that standard is met — adjusting, reassessing, removing, and aligning the necessary people, places, and things in your life.

What is your definition of relationship? Do you desire for intimacy to take a part? I knew long ago for myself, that relationships were something I would not take lightly. If I allowed someone into my space or even if it was, as my Nana would say, flesh of my flesh, blood of my blood, I wanted that relationship to be of substance. I was willing to put a great amount of effort, giving nothing short of what I envisioned relationships to be and what I expected.

I believe we all have the same or similar relationship threads that you'll read about below. I've approached all of these relationships with the standard I've set, some worked out perfectly and others I was sadly disappointed. Either way these relationships taught me priceless lessons, led me to many "In to me see" moments, and sometimes even exposing the toxic places within me that needed to be divorced. I invite you to explore these two core relationship areas that aesthetically make up the essence of connections in many of our lives as believers.

PERMISSION TO PAUSE

Think about what life would look like if we were all more intentional about connecting with one another?

_____

_____

_____

_____

_____

_____

How would your trust grow if you knew you had more deep rooted relationships than surface-level ones?

_____

_____

_____

_____

I want you to pause and think about the relationships you do have and how they'd change if they were approached in a more intimate manner?
What would you do differently?
How do you feel that person would respond?

_____

_____

_____

_____

_____

_____

The Creator (God)

My relationship with God is the best relationship I have ever experienced and will ever have. I have not only built a relationship with God but have intimacy with Him as well. The relationship was the acceptance I longed for while the intimacy was the anchor I needed. Not every relationship I had prior to God has been good. I had some bruises and needed a new foundation. That firm foundation has been the cornerstone for every relationship I now have- knowing that I can't expect anyone to love as pure as Him but I want to do my best to show that kind of love, guidance, support, forgiveness, and endurance that I've been graced with to anyone I can, especially those I'm privileged to be a part of their lives.

True love and relationship with Him has brought about forgiveness, growth, purpose, compassion, wisdom, healing and so much more to my life! My relationship with the Lord has been and will always be the best thing that has ever happened to me. The message of the cross has changed me. The heaviness of my past are now covered through the work of Christ. I can live a FULL life led by the Holy Spirit. I'm forever thankful for reconciliation that I don't even deserve yet I receive!

Key components to a committed relationship with Christ:

1. Accept Him

2. Pray - talk to Him, a dialogue not a monologue

3. Read, Study, and Live His Word

4. Surrender to Him - not my will by Thy Will be Done

God has written love letters throughout the Bible. Letters that would make you think, "why wouldn't I want to be in

relationship with someone who feels this way about me?"
Check out these verses for immediate access to how much He
loves you:

*You did not choose Me, but I chose you and appointed you that you
should go and bear fruit, and that your fruit should remain, that
whatever you ask the Father in My name He may give you.*
John 15:16

*Just as [in His love] He chose us in Christ [actually selected us for
Himself as His own] before the foundation of the world, so that we
would be holy [that is, consecrated, set apart for Him, purpose-
driven] and blameless in His sight.*
Ephesians 1:4 AMP

*Before I formed you in the womb I knew you [and approved of you as
My chosen instrument], And before you were born I consecrated you
[to Myself as My own; I have appointed you as a prophet
to the nations.*
Jeremiah 1:5 AMP

*Bring the ones who are called by My name; the ones I made, shaped,
and created for My profound glory. Isaiah 43:7 VOICE
For I know the plans and thoughts that I have for you,' says the
Lord, 'plans for peace and well-being and not for disaster,
to give you a future and a hope.*
Jeremiah 29:11

*I have loved you with an everlasting love; I have drawn you with
unfailing kindness.*
Jeremiah 31:3

God's love for you is undeniable! After meditating on these scriptures, a strong sense of safety, care, trust, commitment, loyalty, and adoration should overtake you. Which is why I believe your relationship with God is so important. Having this type of reciprocal relationship as your core foundation will position you to live a life of connection and intimacy with God, our Father, Creator, Caregiver, and Protector ; Jesus, our Savior, Redeemer, and Example ; and the Holy Spirit, our Comforter, Guide, and Power.

The Co-Creators (Parents)

Being a parent is a huge responsibility. A life is depending on you as their source of love, nourishment, provision, direction, comfort, stability, safety, emotional and mental support. Even the Bible is clear of the great responsibility of parents:

"Train up a child in the way he should go; even when he is old he will not depart from it."
Proverbs 22:6

"Children are a gift from the Lord; they are a reward from him."
Psalm 127:3

"All your children shall be taught by the Lord, and great shall be the peace of your children."
Isaiah 54:13

"Children's children are a crown to the aged, and parents are the pride of their children."
Proverbs 17:6

"Fathers, do not provoke your children to anger by the way you treat them. Rather, bring them up with the discipline and instruction that comes from the Lord."

Ephesians 6:4

"These commandments that I give you today are to be on your hearts. Impress them on your children. Talk about them when you sit at home and when you walk along the road, when you lie down and when you get up"

Deuteronomy 6:6-7

The relationship you have with your parents has such an influential impact on you and the other relationships you have in life. Some of us were raised with both parents in our lives, others by only one, and some with neither. Through my personal experience of being raised by a single mom, I had this false perception that my friends in two parent homes had this perfect magical experience that I could never have.

Through courageous conversation and an open mind, I learned that many two-parent homes had children who felt like they weren't seen or even had a relationship with a parent that lived in the home with them. That shocked me, but the reality was, no household makeup has the same dynamics. I realized how my blessing really was that I was raised in a home where I never had to question love, safety or provision, a home where I felt and received love on a daily basis, parents who both held me in high regard, raised me to be wise, intelligent and respectful and believed I could achieve anything I put my mind to.

Although my mom's impact resonated deeply because she solely raised me, my father's impact was just as meaningful.

After much healing and processing, I realized the main thing I wanted from my Dad was just more of great things I had experienced with him and a deeper relationship with him.

The enemy wants to keep us stuck in the cycle of toxic feelings, mindsets and behaviors that feed whatever negative narrative we've created about our lives and the people in it. He tried it with me. He tried to drown out who was present by feeding me toxicity on who was absent, wanting me to believe I was unwanted, not good enough, and abandoned; all of which were lies. No one has EVER told me that but that lying devil. I am grateful for my parents and honor them with my life.

Like I shared before, every household dynamic is different. Some of us have been completely abandoned by our biological parent(s) but rescued by the love of foster or bonus parents, while others had to pretend their "big happy family" was great in public but behind closed doors had to sit in the looming atmosphere of divorce.

It's time to work! In the worksheets following this permission to pause we will look at your Relational Blueprints — from early life to adolescence to adulthood as well as set intention for the standard for future relationships.

PERMISSION TO PAUSE

What were your family dynamics like growing up?

_____

_____

_____

_____

_____

_____

_____

_____

_____

_____

How about your relationship with your mom? Dad? Foster/bonus parents or guardians?

_____

_____

_____

_____

_____

_____

_____

_____

_____

_____

YOUR FAMILY DYNAMICS IMPACT AND INFLUENCE YOUR *Healing* MORE THAN YOU KNOW

Relational Blueprint

A RELATIONSHIP TREE WORKSHEET

This worksheet is designed to help you identify the key relationships that have shaped you—your Relational Blueprint. It's not just about blood relatives, but anyone who has significantly impacted your understanding of connection, love, and self. Reflect on each section and fill in the spaces provided.

PART 1: THE ROOTS - Foundations of Connection (Early Life & Family)
Think about the people who raised you or were primary figures in your childhood. What patterns or beliefs about relationships did you learn from them?

PRIMARY CAREGIVERS

Person/Role #1
_____

CORE INFLUENCE
What was their main positive or negative impact?
_____
_____
_____
_____

LESSON LEARNED
What did this relationship teach you about connection?
_____
_____
_____
_____

CURRENT IMPACT
How does this person still affect you today?
_____
_____
_____
_____

PRIMARY CAREGIVERS

Person/Role #2
_____

CORE INFLUENCE
What was their main positive or negative impact?
_____
_____
_____
_____

LESSON LEARNED
What did this relationship teach you about connection?
_____
_____
_____
_____

CURRENT IMPACT
How does this person still affect you today?
_____
_____
_____
_____

Relational Blueprint
A RELATIONSHIP TREE WORKSHEET

This worksheet is designed to help you identify the key relationships that have shaped you—your Relational Blueprint. It's not just about blood relatives, but anyone who has significantly impacted your understanding of connection, love, and self. Reflect on each section and fill in the spaces provided.

PART 2: THE TRUNK- Growing & Changing (Adolescence & Young Adulthood
Consider significant friendships, mentors, or early romantic relationships. How did these connections help you understand yourself and others during formative years?

SIGNIFICANT PERSON	SIGNIFICANT PERSON
Person/Role #5	Person/Role #6
CORE INFLUENCE What was their main positive or negative impact?	**CORE INFLUENCE** What was their main positive or negative impact?
LESSON LEARNED What did this relationship teach you about connection?	**LESSON LEARNED** What did this relationship teach you about connection?
CURRENT IMPACT How does this person still affect you today?	**CURRENT IMPACT** How does this person still affect you today?

Relational Blueprint
A RELATIONSHIP TREE WORKSHEET

This worksheet is designed to help you identify the key relationships that have shaped you—your Relational Blueprint. It's not just about blood relatives, but anyone who has significantly impacted your understanding of connection, love, and self. Reflect on each section and fill in the spaces provided.

PART 3: THE BRANCHES- Current Connections (Adult Life)
Consider significant friendships, mentors, or early romantic relationships. How did these connections help you understand yourself and others during formative years?

SIGNIFICANT PERSON

Person/Role #7 (e.g., Spouse, Partner, Closest Friend)

_____

CORE INFLUENCE
What was their main positive or negative impact?

_____
_____
_____

LESSON LEARNED
What did this relationship teach you about connection?

_____
_____
_____

CURRENT IMPACT
How does this person still affect you today?

_____
_____
_____

SIGNIFICANT PERSON

Person/Role #8 (e.g., Spouse, Partner, Closest Friend)

_____

CORE INFLUENCE
What was their main positive or negative impact?

_____
_____
_____

LESSON LEARNED
What did this relationship teach you about connection?

_____
_____
_____

CURRENT IMPACT
How does this person still affect you today?

_____
_____
_____

Relational Blueprint
A RELATIONSHIP TREE WORKSHEET

This worksheet is designed to help you identify the key relationships that have shaped you—your Relational Blueprint. It's not just about blood relatives, but anyone who has significantly impacted your understanding of connection, love, and self. Reflect on each section and fill in the spaces provided.

PART 4: THE FRUIT- Intentional Cultivation (Your Future Relationships)
Based on your reflections, what changes do you want to make to your Relational Blueprint moving forward?

SELF REFLECTION

One key insight about your relationships you discovered through this tree:

_____
_____
_____
_____

One unhealthy pattern you commit to pruning:

_____
_____
_____
_____

One healthy connection you commit to nurturing:

_____
_____
_____
_____

Your prayer for your future relationships, guided by God:

_____
_____
_____
_____
_____

Now that you've completed that course of the journey, I want you to take two of those relationships that impact you the most and complete the Assessing Our Relationships worksheets. For each attribute listed, rate your experience on a scale of 1 to 5, then total your score.

Healthy Scoring

A score of **0–15 suggests a Fragmented Foundation**, where past wounds may still be drowning out your ability to connect and see this person through the eyes of God; this is a sacred invitation to silence the past and rebuild on Truth. A score of **16–30 indicates a Developing Connection**, where trust is growing but lingering bruises still affect your ability to fully receive. If you score between **31–45, you are experiencing Solid Reciprocity**, moving beyond survival and beginning to trust and love again from your new foundation. Finally, a score of **46–50 reflects an Intimate Core**, where you are walking in the fullness of healing and your relationship is a surrendered work of art, that aligns with the heart of God.

Unhealthy Scoring

A score of **0–15 suggests Walking in Freedom**, where these unhealthy patterns no longer have a foothold and you are moving in the light of God's truth. A score of **16–30 indicates Emerging Awareness**, where you are beginning to identify the bruises of the past but they still may whisper lies to your heart. If you score between **31–45, you are experiencing Hindering Patterns**, where old habits and unhealed trauma are actively blocking the intimacy you were created for. Finally, a score of **46–50 reflects Deep Strongholds**, representing areas where the enemy has built a fortress that requires intentional, total surrender to the Father's healing touch.

Assessing Our Relationships
WORKSHEET

Over the course of our time together, we have determined what constitutes a healthy/unhealthy relationship. Use this worksheet to further assess valuable or questionable relationships in your life.

_____
Name, Who/what they are to you

HEALTHY

TRUST
☆ ☆ ☆ ☆ ☆

COMMUNICATION
☆ ☆ ☆ ☆ ☆

RESPECT
☆ ☆ ☆ ☆ ☆

UNDERSTANDING
☆ ☆ ☆ ☆ ☆

ACCOUNTABILITY
☆ ☆ ☆ ☆ ☆

SECURITY
☆ ☆ ☆ ☆ ☆

HONESTY
☆ ☆ ☆ ☆ ☆

EMPATHY
☆ ☆ ☆ ☆ ☆

FAITH/GOD
☆ ☆ ☆ ☆ ☆

LOVE
☆ ☆ ☆ ☆ ☆

_____ /50 stars
Count the # of total stars and place the number above

Total Your Score:
45–50: Abiding Intimacy | 30–44: Consistent Connection
15–29: Emerging Trust | Below 15: A Season for Surrender

UNHEALTHY

UNRESOLVED ISSUES
☆ ☆ ☆ ☆ ☆

LACK OF GRACE
☆ ☆ ☆ ☆ ☆

UNFORGIVENESS
☆ ☆ ☆ ☆ ☆

MANIPULATIONS
☆ ☆ ☆ ☆ ☆

DEMEANING
☆ ☆ ☆ ☆ ☆

LYING
☆ ☆ ☆ ☆ ☆

DISTRUST
☆ ☆ ☆ ☆ ☆

DISRESPECT
☆ ☆ ☆ ☆ ☆

UNSATISFIED
☆ ☆ ☆ ☆ ☆

COMPLAINING
☆ ☆ ☆ ☆ ☆

UNEQUALLY YOKED
☆ ☆ ☆ ☆ ☆

_____ /50 stars
Count the # of total stars and place the number above

Total Your Score:
45–50: Deep Strongholds | 30–44: Hindering Patterns
15–29: Emerging Awareness | Below 15: Walking in Freedom

Assessing Our Relationships
WORKSHEET

Over the course of our time together, we have determined what constitutes a healthy / unhealthy relationship. Use this worksheet to further assess valuable or questionable relationships in your life.

_____
Name, Who/what they are to you

HEALTHY

TRUST
☆ ☆ ☆ ☆ ☆

COMMUNICATION
☆ ☆ ☆ ☆ ☆

RESPECT
☆ ☆ ☆ ☆ ☆

UNDERSTANDING
☆ ☆ ☆ ☆ ☆

ACCOUNTABILITY
☆ ☆ ☆ ☆ ☆

SECURITY
☆ ☆ ☆ ☆ ☆

HONESTY
☆ ☆ ☆ ☆ ☆

EMPATHY
☆ ☆ ☆ ☆ ☆

FAITH/GOD
☆ ☆ ☆ ☆ ☆

LOVE
☆ ☆ ☆ ☆ ☆

_____ /50 stars

Count the # of total stars and place the number above

Total Your Score:
45–50: Abiding Intimacy | 30–44: Consistent Connection
15–29: Emerging Trust | Below 15: A Season for Surrender

UNHEALTHY

UNRESOLVED ISSUES
☆ ☆ ☆ ☆ ☆

LACK OF GRACE
☆ ☆ ☆ ☆ ☆

UNFORGIVENESS
☆ ☆ ☆ ☆ ☆

MANIPULATIONS
☆ ☆ ☆ ☆ ☆

DEMEANING
☆ ☆ ☆ ☆ ☆

LYING
☆ ☆ ☆ ☆ ☆

DISTRUST
☆ ☆ ☆ ☆ ☆

DISRESPECT
☆ ☆ ☆ ☆ ☆

UNSATISFIED
☆ ☆ ☆ ☆ ☆

COMPLAINING
☆ ☆ ☆ ☆ ☆

UNEQUALLY YOKED
☆ ☆ ☆ ☆ ☆

_____ /50 stars

Count the # of total stars and place the number above

Total Your Score:
45–50: Deep Strongholds | 30–44: Hindering Patterns
15–29: Emerging Awareness | Below 15: Walking in Freedom

Mindset Matters

"Your beliefs become your thoughts, your thoughts become your words, your words become your actions, your actions become your habits, your habits become your values, your values become your destiny."
—Mahatma Gandhi

The relationships we develop, our experiences, perception, and view of those relationship shapes many of our mindsets. The definition of mindset is *a mental attitude or inclination a fixed state of mind.* Your mindset is your collection of thoughts and beliefs that shape your thought habits. And your thoughts and habits affect how you think, what you feel, and what you do. Your mindset impacts how you make sense of the world, and how you make sense of you.

Proverbs 23:7 says, "As a man thinks in his heart, so is he." So, we see the power our thoughts and mindset have on our identity, which is vitally important to your healing journey. We'll have to get rid of mindsets that don't serve us and prepare ourselves with mindsets that align with God, our purpose, the victories we've won, and our future.

There is said to be 3 types of mindsets: Fixed, Growth, Benefit *(www.benefitmindset.com).* A fixed mindset seeks perfection and avoids failure. They focus on what they know and believe their strengths can't be developed so they focus on perfecting their abilities. A growth mindset seeks growth and development. They focus on how to improve what they do and believe their strengths can be developed with effort, skill, and ability. A benefit mindset builds on the growth mindset and is one who seeks to be well and do good. They focus on why they do what they do and believes in developing their strengths and intentionally contributing to the good.

While identifying the mindset types is beneficial, there is a primary mindset we live by as believers and that is a kingdom mindset. It comes from Matthew 6:10 (TPT): "Manifest your kingdom realm, and cause your every purpose to be fulfilled on earth, just as it is fulfilled in heaven." We are ambassadors of the kingdom of God which represents change, truth, power, love and redemption. We carry a mindset that is reflective of the mind of Christ. Here are some scriptural tools you can use to further build on your Kingdom Mindset:

- Ephesians 4:22-23 (AMP)
- Colossians 3:2 (AMP)
- Philippians 2:2-5 (NKJV / AMP)
- Romans 8:5-6
- Philippians 4:8
- Romans 1: 28-32 (AMP / NKJV)

We've made it to the close of relationships and mindsets on our journey. You have learned about the hurt, the healing, and how relationships and mindsets play a huge part on our experiences both past and future. Now we're equipped with a proper perspective to assess and restore our relationships and mindsets to better posture us for the rest of the journey.

Now let's head down the road to finish up this Beauty and Bruised phase by divorcing the things that can't come with you in Phase 2: Beauty and the Blessed.

Dear Healing

Thank you for the courage to tell my story from the lens of purpose not pain. My vulnerability has met The Savior's redemption, and I am thankful!

PERMISSION TO PAUSE

What kind of mindset do you have? What has contributed to that mindset?

_____

_____

_____

_____

_____

_____

Considering your healing journey, what kind of mindset do you need?

_____

_____

_____

_____

What can you do to develop this mindset?

_____

_____

_____

_____

_____

_____

_____

_____

_____

REAL... RAW... TOXIC!

4

DIVORCING ME

Early one morning, about 2 am, I found myself in the bathroom talking to God about a heart matter. As I asked for guidance on how to navigate and handle my emotions regarding the situation, this is what the conversation was like:

God: What about you?

Me: Yes. . .What about me?

God: Here's a lesson for you... everything doesn't have to be done your way and your way isn't always the best way. If wisdom were leading, it would be knowledgeable of various solutions and be able to make a sound choice out of all of them. Wisdom just wouldn't pick what it wants and be done!

Me: (3 blinks and a blank stare) Okay I mean it makes sense... note taken! So what do I do about this situation?

God: Do you realize that it is okay to have strong love and mixed emotions at the same time?

Me: (Blank stare...thinking where's He going with this?)

God: When you accept this as possible, you can free yourself of feeling it is wrong. These powerful entities, love and emotions, don't appear to be working together but they are both very much a part of the growth process.

Me: Ummmmm, okay that's deep. Guess I need to work on that too. The lessons during this season tell me something must have been off with what I was doing.

God: This season is called "Divorcing Me." In this season you will separate from the toxic mindsets and behaviors you have functioned in throughout your life.

Me: Woooooooow that's different! Okay God!

God: You need to write that down and look up the definition.

A lot, right? So let me give a little context to the space I was in when this happened. The year 2019 was full of favor; things that I have been praying for over decades began to appear. I was utterly in awe of how God was showing off in my life, yet with the favor came greater responsibility and challenges. One difficult challenge was realizing all these blessings I knew were in reach were not quite ready for me to obtain yet. I knew I asked for it, reserved it, even put a down payment on it, but I could not have them yet. I was in an interesting space of learning how to be aware and sometimes even experience the goodness over my life, yet also growing to a new level of patience and faith to wait on it until it was in full blossom.

Here is what I found as I journeyed within my 2 a.m. divorce session with God. According to Merriam- Webster Dictionary online, divorce is:

Legal dissolution of a marriage by a court or other competent body (In this case God Almighty Himself) To legally dissolve one's marriage; To separate or dissociate from something. Synonyms: official separation, disunion, break up, split up, estrangement, alienation, disconnect, detach.

After writing down and processing the true meaning of divorce in regard to my situation, I was floored. I was coming to God to fix them but He revealed how I was the cause of what I was blaming on someone else. In that moment I realized that the process of Divorcing Me was a serious task.

My parents were never married, and I've actually never been in close connection with anyone who has had a divorce. I just knew a lot from Tyler Perry movies (laughing to myself) – divorces did not usually end well; they were full of strife, drama, hurt, and pain which typically had negative effects on families. I knew that when I got married, a divorce wasn't going to be an option.

Honestly, I thought divorce was a story I couldn't tell or even give insight on due to my inexperience. As I sat on my bed with my journal I wrote at the top of a new page "Toxic Mindsets/Behaviors." Within a good 15 minutes I had a list of ten items listed. The way they came so easily and were laid out in bullet points with descriptions in my journal was a sure indicator that this "Divorcing Me" season was bigger than me. Through the nausea in my stomach, the tears streaming down my face, and the tremble of my hands I wrote and sat with some of the ugliest, most embarrassing parts of me.

I looked at this journal entry, which looked pretty similar to a book outline, I knew that divorcing the deep dark parts of me and allowing this process to cleanse and heal me were

WHY I WANTED

Out!!!

going to cleanse and heal a lot of other people in the same way. I shut my journal, laid in my bed and said, "God, I commit myself to going through with this divorce. I'm so sorry I've acted this way for all of these years. I really cannot believe that you continued to bless me and love me even when I showed up this way, even when you knew these deep parts of me exist. I don't want anyone connected to me, especially anyone I love to experience any of these toxic behaviors from me. I WANT OUT!"

The next morning, I woke up sobbing… It was Mother's Day. I had plans to go to church then hang out with my mom, but I literally felt depression sitting heavy on me. I didn't want to get out of bed. I laid there for 3 hours sobbing. I didn't want to eat, go to the bathroom, and I definitely didn't want to leave my house. I mustered up the strength to make my Mother's Day Facebook posts for my mom and sister, yet little did people know I was completely wrecked as I wrote. I was trying to figure out if I was feeling someone else's grief, if I was going through some crazy whacked out hormonal change, or if I was sad because I was a 33 year old woman sitting in a home alone on Mother's Day without any children, even though I should have two. (I will explain more about this later in a toxic mindset).

My emotions were everywhere yet I was getting nowhere on why I felt so horrible. I was close to just disappointing my family so I could just sulk in my feelings. Then a new conversation started:

God: It's time to get up and get in the shower.

Me: (crying) I don't want to. I want to stay here! What is this?!?!?

God: DIVORCE

Me: (Face palm)

God: When that which was once loved, common and embraced is severed it causes great pain and anguish. Marriage is meant to make two become one. Imagine how it would feel to somehow find a way to separate what has been meshed together. You're grieving the heaviness, guilt, and shame are normal feelings of a divorce.

Me: (blank stare) Maybe I don't want to do this.

God: You want to continue to live with those toxic mindsets you wrote down?

Me: No but I feel so horrible that I've exposed so many people, destroyed so many relationships, hacked away at my self-worth and value. Some of these mindsets have robbed me of blessings and the faith that I'll ever get blessed in that way again.

God: This isn't a punishment. This is an opportunity for you to take charge over your life and eliminate these things from it so I can add more blessings and purpose.

I finally cried my way to the shower, but my tears shifted. They weren't tears of shame but the overwhelming love, patience, and partnership of God for the ugly journey. I knew I wouldn't be walking alone. God would be with me and somehow through this mess, something beyond beautiful, meant for His glory, was going to be birthed in me bring God.

The Rebel — "I Do What I Want To Do"

There has to be a fine line between independence and this toxic mindset. For a long time, I embraced it all as independence. I was raised by a strong black woman who did it all on her own. My big sister was also a strong black woman who raised her children, met her goals and lived the life she wanted. I mean I was surrounded by the make it happen, go get what you want, independent women and I looked up to them in my life. My relational blueprint showed up as I imitated and became a woman who knows what she wants and doesn't have to wait on others to make life happen.

I think the problem came when I started to take my independence too far, almost like a sense of entitlement. As my mom would say, "You're getting carried away with yourself now!" Carried away was right! I became so used to "doing my own thang" and doing it pretty well. I would set a goal and accomplish it, with much hard work and dedication. I was blessed with multiple choices and opportunities in life and usually find myself on the right side of my decisions. All of the right moves made me confident in my ability to call the shots and make sound decisions in my life.

As a woman of faith who relies heavily on the leading of God, I recall myself saying on numerous occasions "God trusts me to make this decision," which is backwards when the Bible tells us to trust in the Lord and lean not unto our own understanding (Proverbs 3:5). This confidence had me fully embracing this "I do what I want" mindset. Pretty much whatever I felt contributed to my overall growth and life desires; I could and would obtain it. I heard so many people say, "Why am I wasting my breath? You're going to do what you want anyway!"

And they were right. As I grew more mature, I would listen to others' opinions or thoughts, but at the end of the day, I was going to do what I felt was best for me, or just what I wanted to do at the moment.

How would one recognize this "I do what I want" mindset within themselves? Well the mindset is extremely selfish, self-absorbed and self-motivated, often found breaking rules or making their own, closed-minded and centered on their way, bossy, resistant, and/or demanding, vocal and at times defensive about their choices, and willing to eliminate any barriers in the way of what they want.

I know, I know… you're saying to yourself "Not Soleil! She's so sweet!" Well, I'm here to tell you YES, the person described above was me in more ways than one. I believe this mindset went from independent to toxic during one big life decision back in 2002. I honestly wasn't at the legal age to make the decision I made nor mature enough to make a wise decision independently. I remember like it was yesterday talking myself into it. "Listen you can't allow anything to get in the way of your plan. Get rid of whatever is in your way!"

In 2002, my junior year of high school, I found out I was pregnant by my no-good boyfriend. During that time, I had everyone practically convinced I was an angel. I went to church, got excellent grades, was involved in student and community activities, sang in the choir, mimed and would soon be college bound. Not many people knew of one of my biggest goals during high school, which was to avoid getting pregnant in my teenage years. I had vowed to break the generational curse, and of course my rebel nature, eliminating barriers, enabled me to live that out by any means necessary.

This "I do what I want" rebel mindset ruled me. All of the descriptions fit me! I eliminated all barriers in the way of my goal, which was to finish high school and go to college without children. In my mind, having a child was a barrier, and I had to eliminate it. Even though I was underage, and it was against what I was taught, the "I do what I want" mindset took over; I had an abortion.

Mentally I had convinced myself it was the best thing to do as I replayed the barriers and my goal on repeat in my mind:

- "I vowed to not have a child young and technically I'm not!"

- "I have a bright future, I can't let a baby get in the way!"

- "I don't want my child to grow up without a father in their life. I have to break this generational cycle!"

Physically, it was one of the most invasive painful things I have ever been through. I was haunted by my own whimpers at night and the sounds of the machines for years. Even though I made it through my teenage years without a child, graduated high school with honors and scholarships, and successfully completed college, at night no one knew the pain and resentment deep within me. This toxic mindset invited me to a place of selfishness because it invited a fear and expectation for consequences that followed me constantly. I was afraid I'd be punished by not being able to conceive when I was ready to have a child, afraid I would have complications due to my poor choices. It wasn't until I reestablished my relationship with God that I began facing those fears and anxieties. Yet even if I had conquered that mountain of guilt, resentment and disbelief connected to the abortion, that mindset wasn't addressed.

So often we address circumstances and situations but fail to address the root issue which is necessary for complete healing. So, the "toxic rebel, do what you want mindset" would still surface in my life. I had forgiven myself for the abortion and even able to share my testimony with other young women facing or recovering from that same decision.

We convince ourselves that if we're helping someone else through shared ecperiences, then we've done well. That is indeed a great accomplishment, yet God is concerned about the state of our hearts. We often we push all that energy to helping others and we are dying on the inside — living with deep seated unresolved issues. The rebel in me remained. It reared its head in every area of my life – church, family, friends, work, relationships, and more.

I realized that in order to free myself I had to trace my steps back to the origin of this rebel nature. I had to stare that selfish, self-centered, bossy teenager in the face and tell her that self centered mindset has no place in our future. I had to be honest with myself and acknowledge that I had allowed selfishness to grip me up for too long in life. I sat with the effects it had on my decision making as well as on the people in my life. I had to admit I was guilty of justifying wrong in order to feel right. I had to ask for forgiveness for those who I had hurt with this behavior. I had to forgive and free myself from that mindset and speak into who I am and believed God had called me to be.

DIVORCE DECLARATION

I AM NO LONGER A REBEL!

I am divorced from this toxic mindset and disassociate myself with any past rebellious behavior. I curse any memories of this behavior with intentions to taunt or paralyze me in my heart, mind, body, and soul and speak everything good over my life –restoration and perfect peace!

STATEMENT OF IDENTITY

I AM LOVE AND LIGHT…

and love does not demand its own way.
It leads me wherever I go.
The source of my light is from God and I am continuously powered by it. The Holy Spirit is my guide and I will follow as He directs me - without hesitation, without doubt, and without fear.

The Pedestal Problem — "I Deserve"

Webster says, "Deserve is used when a person should rightly receive something good or bad because of his or her actions or character."

After hearing my friends and family say it countless times, year after year I began to believe it. I heard the words, "You deserve…" in almost every area of life from relationships, the workplace, mentors and mentees, church, education, and more, its frequency begin to confirm its alleged truth. All of my life I've heard how much I deserved this or that—I deserved that scholarship or promotion or award or recognition. I deserved to have a good man, the life I desired, the ability to go and travel the world, the house and multiple cars I bought, every blessing and success that comes my way and even the world.

Let's talk about how this "I deserve" mindset can take a wrong turn and how you can spot this pedestal problem. As stated earlier after hearing anything repeatedly, you began to believe it. What you speak takes root in you and begins to absorb your self-perception along with how others view you, eventually growing into what you think, speak or beleive about yourself. This "I deserve" mindset can evolve into a strong sense of entitlement. Because "I deserve", everything should go my way, everyone should make sure I'm comfortable and happy especially since I'm doing all these "good things". This mindset can distort your view, making you feel as if you're "elevated" or "higher" than others. It is again another self-centered and misleading mindset.

I recall a time when my "I deserve" mindset haunted me. I was in a "situationship" with a guy and over time he grew on me. One thing about me is I love VERY hard and once I let you in, it's quite the task to get you out of my system. At that point in my life, I strongly desired love and to continue the connection I had with this man. My friends and family saw the "situationship" or better known on the Red Table Talk as "entanglement" differently. They expressed to me that I deserved better, that I didn't deserve to be used or taken advantage of. They didn't believe this man deserved to be with me yet based on my personal feelings for him, I did.

My friends flat out said "We want something different for you. A man that won't be afraid to commit to you and love you." I heard my girls out, acknowledged some truths in what they said but unfortunately my desire overshadowed the truth they were presenting to me. Yes, I became a woman so far gone she couldn't even see how bad and unhealthy the situation really was.

I was bound to learn the hard way. I called myself being patient with this man and his needs for several years and chose to stand on broken promises for this "love" we would share. It wasn't until that man practically told me, "I put you on a pedestal and viewed you with such regard that I don't feel as if I deserve you." I was baffled and confused, and sitting in a pool of "I told you so's" that confirmed all the red flags my friends and family raised. How is it that I was so caught up in the "I deserve with a splash of I do what I want" mindset that others saw my value more than me, even the man that broke my heart!!

In my mind, I deserved love and happiness. I manipulated how I viewed that relationship so much so that I believed I was getting that, when I wasn't. When he told me that, I was furious. I didn't ask to be on a pedestal; I asked to be loved and chosen. I didn't ask him to decide he didn't deserve me; I just wanted him to see I loved and accepted him and was willing to grow through the good and the bad with him. The pedestal was great when the perspective provided praise, comfort and blessings yet when the viewpoint from the pedestal revealed a land full of the bitter truth, embarrassment, disappointment, and false hope that pedestal became problematic — was it good or bad?

This is why this mindset is toxic. It entices you into believing that whatever you believe you deserve is good for you even if it isn't God's best for you. The sense of entitlement can be so intense that you're so stuck on what you deserve that you're too blind to see that person, place or thing doesn't deserve you.

Our mind can be compared to a helium balloon that has been over pumped with so many "I deserve this" and "You deserve better than that" statements that we become so prideful and elevated in those thoughts that prevent us from seeing the situation clearly. We can rise so high, eventually causing explosion from the excessive pressure. This "I deserve" mindset will sweep you and your rationality, wisdom, value, and standards away. This mindset had me believing I was higher than I was, when in some instances I was settling for less than I deserved.

As a child of God, I acknowledge Him as my source, yet somehow, I took pride in feeling like I had something to do with the favor on my life. Finding myself confidently wrong in a toxic situation where my own decision making and choices rooted in "I know what's right and I deserve!", wrecked me. This mindset is unhealthy. In order to come into my full purpose of absorbing who God says I am with all humility and glory given to Him; I needed to divorce the "I deserve" mindset.

DIVORCE DECLARATION

I AM NO LONGER ON A PEDESTAL

I am divorced from this toxic mindset and disassociate myself with any past prideful behavior. I curse any memories of this behavior with intentions to taunt or paralyze me in my heart, mind, body, and soul and speak everything good over my life –humility and surrender!

STATEMENT OF IDENTITY

MY LIFE IS GRACED BY GOD...

and grace is undeserved favor. I walk in complete grace, humility and gratitude in God's plan for me. Those toxic behaviors should disqualify me from His love and blessings but instead He accepts, rebuilds, and restores me, giving me what He believes I deserve and nothing less. God is the only one on a pedestal in my life! I will never again dethrone God from my life's pedestal and take His rightful seat. As I exalt Him, He will add to me!

The Entitled One - I Want It My Way Now

Growing up, I was often referred to as spoiled, and something about it never sat well with me. My idea of "spoiled" was someone who demanded what they wanted and got it most, if not every time. A spoiled person was self-centered and self-absorbed, excessively catered to, whiny and irrational with their requests. I often think of Veruca Salt the spoiled little girl in the movie "Willy Wonka and the Chocolate Factory."

Veruca was the epitome of a spoiled brat, she would make her demands and her father would say things like, "Anything you want sweetheart! You can have all those things when we get home." Veruca even had a song in the movie entitled "I want it now!" She would say things like "Give it to me now!" Or "And if I don't get the things I'm after I'm going to scream. I don't care how; I want it now!" When I heard the word spoiled, her face flashed in my mind, and I personally never thought I showed behaviors similar to Veruca.

I felt like someone who acted like Veruca was annoying, ungrateful, and entitled. I would argue my mom down about calling me spoiled. I would ask her, "How am I spoiled? I definitely don't get everything I want or ask for."

My mom would reply, "But you ask and if I could, I would give it to you." I still didn't perceive that as spoiled because the whole process I envisioned wasn't happening – I wasn't getting everything I wanted or asked for, and I definitely wasn't demanding, but I've never had an issue asking for what I want.

I was in denial. I may not be on the level of Veruca, but there were tendencies in me, and what I learned is that my spoiled nature was heavily defined by how others treated me. In the Divorcing Me chapter, I had a dialogue with God that introduced this spoiled rotten mindset I had. I was seeking understanding from God on why someone wasn't responding or communicating to me in a "proper" way (I say proper in that way because it was just improper from my perspective). I'm telling God how it made me feel, how I want to feel, and asking Him what I should do (lots of self-centered actions here).

God began to show me myself in that moment. After telling me "Love doesn't demand its own way", He said "You're a nice manipulator!" Now that took me out of here because similarly to being called spoiled, I would never imagine being manipulative. He further explained "You have people eating out of your hand, wanting to give you the world and will do anything for you. The problem is you use that to your advantage – the motive behind your requests and demands are self-serving!"

Well alright!! I had to do a lot of self-examination and processing to receive that but after looking at my life and recalling some repetitive comments from multiple people, I realized that I was guilty.

At a young age I learned how to get what I wanted using a huge smile and my big pretty brown eyes to my advantage or negotiating to get my desires fulfilled. I was often the child that couldn't just let good works be, I needed something in return. I couldn't just wash the dishes; I needed to know that if I washed the dishes then I would be getting this or that. Now don't get me wrong, I was a sweet girl, my mom didn't nickname me "Lovey" for no reason! I was full of love, light and sunshine and I was a good girl.

My mother raised me to listen, have manners, be kind,

respectful and treat others how I wished to be treated. Being sweet and good only complicated this notion of being spoiled. It almost fed the monster because I felt like "I Deserved" (we've explored that road already) what I asked for since I was such a great girl. Yet that conditional mindset played into this spoiled behavior. Using my charm and lovey-ness to get what I wanted was manipulation.

Another thing I realized is that those who fall victim to our manipulative ways are typically the ones that we love the most—the ones closest to you to get the deepest wounds. I would say growing up being spoiled had its innocence especially since the people who experienced it loved me in a such a way that they wanted to provide everything I asked for, but as I became an adult I realized this behavior would negatively flow into relationships.

I can't tell you how many times I heard from a man I was dealing with, "It's your world Soleil; I'm just in it!" While that may sound great if you twist it to mean that the man was ready to give me the world and all I wanted and needed (which is a stretch). In actuality it's a loaded statement not rooted in the unity meant for relationships, but the acceptance of a man's sarcasm or tolerance of a spoiled woman.

My degree in Communications. I've grown to treasure healthy communication as one of the biggest building blocks in any successful relationship. As I matured, my view and desire in relationships did. I felt myself desiring a more shared experience in a relationship. I didn't want a man to just live in my world but our world. I wanted to be told no sometimes, that actually became attractive to me to have a man that can show his ability to discern what's best for me/us, not just give me what I want. I found this in a few relationships but realized that the manipulation and spoiled rotten mindset had deeper roots.

While a man could help me see other ways, that did not rescue him from the manipulation games I played to get what I want. It also didn't spare me from the bruises of my own manipulative ways. Have you ever heard of someone manipulating love? I was a master manipulator. Being spoiled empowered me to tailor relationships to keep me satisfied. I mean I would have men that I knew didn't meet the standard of man I desired but they had a purpose – whether it be companionship or cuddle buddy as we'd like to call it, or intellectual enticement that fed my mind but did nothing for my spirit.

I had men that I wanted to give my heart to fully. I saw potential in them, shared a genuine connection and was ready to be in a relationship. Whatever the plot, I would roll out my charm, beauty, lovey-ness, sweet and encouraging spirit just to pull them in tight which usually worked without any issue. That alone would make them want to give me what I wanted, and I was "happy." But I wasn't truly happy because remember I said I was maturing in what I desired from relationships? Well I was, so it'd never fail to pan out this way, I'd set my intention for a relationship, which wasn't much because most men I dealt with didn't know what they wanted anyway. So I could play games and get what I wanted. It went left when what I truly wanted which waws companionship and love, surfaced as new intentions.

I found myself hitting a brick wall trying to manipulate someone into loving me beyond the expectations that were set. It worked for little things, likely because they were beneficial to them. The minute I'd act like I had a standard or wanted more things would go wrong. And instead of allowing what they showed me to be enough to walk away I started to take my spoiled rotten, I want it now, manipulative ways to dangerous levels. I began to make myself think that these relationships were more than what they were. I would cling onto any action, word, promise, or glimmer of hope that man would offer in hopes to salvage what I had invested in hopes that it would transpire into something more.

When being spoiled and having it your way gets to a place where you're manipulating your own thoughts and behavior, you are in severe trouble. I say it all the time that our energy is better spent on what we can control, and WE have the greatest control over ourselves, not others. So, when I practice what I preach and look at how poor my self-control has been at the expense of being spoiled, I knew it was time for change. The facades I built in my mind about relationships were fake. I was living a lie because I needed to have it my way. I think back to all I may have sacrificed by embracing this mindset and everyone who I had scarred and left confused because of it. The conflict within was hard because I knew the better that I wanted but I was so used to controlling the situation to get a replica of it but certainly not the real thing.

If you're anything like me and have lived with this disappointing and mentally exhausting mindset, then you're desperate to be free. How can we experience what true love and companionship is when everything is all about us?

DIVORCE DECLARATION

I AM NO LONGER DEMANDING MY WAY!

I am divorced from this toxic mindset and disassociate myself with any past selfish behavior. I curse any memories of this behavior with intentions to taunt or paralyze me in my heart, mind, body, and soul and speak everything good over my life –unity and selflessness!

STATEMENT OF IDENTITY

I GIVE MYSELF PERMISSION...

to be free to be loved and to give love in an equitable and pure way. I welcome sharing my world with those I love opposed to manipulating situations to serve me. I will be wise enough not to strip myself of the beautiful traits about me just because I 've used them improperly but will embrace the grace extended to use every part of me to bring honor and glory to God.

Discounted Doll - Internalizing External Issues

I don't know any child who goes into a store and doesn't ask for something. That brings me back to my childhood, when my mom used to take me to my favorite stores, precisely any store with a toy aisle. I always wanted either a new doll or something artsy to take home. My momma raised me to be a smart shopper which meant looking for the sale tags and always checking the clearance aisle first. That woman is a God send – I live by the smart shopper rule to this day.

Anyway, I remember I'd look for the sale coupons and sometimes the best Barbie with a bike and a little dog would be the special sale and other times in the clearance aisle I'd see a baby doll whose box looked really rough like someone had dropped it, opened it, then shoved it in and put it back on the shelf but the doll seemed okay. I've always been a curious one and loaded with questions for my mom, so I'd ask, "Why is this AWESOME Barbie with the bike and dog on sale? Shouldn't it be expensive? What happened to that baby doll? The box looks raggedy so I don't want it!"

She'd answer, "Sometimes stores just have deals on great items or they order too many, so they place them on sale. It could be that boxes get messed up when they unload their shipments, or people take things home and return them. Just because the box is rough doesn't mean the doll isn't just fine."

I would have never thought my pleasant experience doll shopping would correlate to a toxic mindset I would have to free myself from one day. As life happened and the cards I had been dealt spread, I had a plethora of amazing experiences but equally if not more experiences of neglect, disappointment, inadequacies, and unworthiness which caused me to be curious and explore. I wanted to know why to a lot of deeper issues that mommy couldn't answer easily and didn't necessarily have an answer for.

As a maturing girl, I wanted to know why my dad didn't spend time with me. Why didn't he call to check on me? Why do I only hear from him on my birthday, when school is starting back, and maybe Christmas? When would my first daddy/daughter date would be? Why don't I know my Dad's side of my family like I do my mom's side? Then as I matured into a young woman exploring relationships and friendships more unanswered questions came. I've been blessed to have some of the most solid friends with whom I shared over three decades of friendship with, yet there were some questionable friends and associates along the way.

I found myself frequently asking questions like this as a teenager and even into adulthood. Why is she being funny toward me when we were just hanging out? Why did she share my business with her other friends? Why didn't I get invited? Why doesn't she like me all of a sudden? Why does she have a problem with me, and I didn't do anything? Why is she comparing herself to me all of the time?

Then moving into relationships, I found a ton of questions as well that stemmed from teenage to adulthood years. Why is he treating me like this? Why does he act differently in public than he does when it is just us? Why is he sending me confusing and mixed messages? Why does it feel like he's hiding me? Why does it seem like all he wants is my body but no real connection or commitment? Why did he lie about his job, his girlfriend/wife, or what he wants from me? Why does he say he loves God but surely doesn't act like it or treat me like it? Why did he ghost me? Why do men play the most games? Why can't they just be honest with their feelings? Why did he switch up on me after all the time and energy I invested?

I can go on and on, but as you can see, I had a lot of questions. Now remember I'm naturally a pretty bold person, so I have asked some of these questions in hopes to gain understanding yet most of the time the answer never justified the treatment and confusion I sat with. I tried to figure out the answers myself.

I practiced self-reflection because I am well aware that the one I can control most effectively is myself. Self-reflection caused me to dig deeper into the issue. So, I began to wonder… What is wrong with me? Did I do something to cause this treatment? What can I do differently? And the process of already carrying the hurt and confusion all these questions caused along with trying to seek closure and understanding on my own, I began to internalize these questions and point the blame back to myself because I can control me.

I became the "Discounted Doll," which in most cases there was nothing major wrong with it, but external factors were causing her to be discounted. Now the Barbie and baby dolls went home with a happy little girl. But the "Discounted Doll" who is a full-blown mature woman doesn't get to go home to anyone, she sits wondering why she's been on the shelf for so long waiting to be treated well and loved right. She begins to measure her worth by the way people treat her even if she shows up and feels every bit of sunshine and happiness within her. Why? Because she's thoroughly confused on how one can show so much love and be kind yet still cycle through the puzzling questions of why people treated her this way.

For years I had internalized not having my expectation of the "ideal father" in my life. I wanted to blame him, but I also wanted his love more so I held onto the blame I wanted to project on him in hopes it would produce the love I desired. That mindset and behavior as a little girl carried onto relationships especially with men. I would find myself making excuses for their behavior, trying to keep hope alive at the expense of my standards, worth and value. I was not blind to the undeserved treatment or wrong thing they did toward me, I just allowed it to discount my worth instead of making moves that showed I truly wanted more for myself. The asinine thing is, my Dad was being the best dad he knew how to be all along. As stated earlier, I realized through healing that I just wanted more of the love and attention I did receive from him growing up and for it to measure up to the amount my mom gave me causing me to overflow with love.

Nonetheless my dad was never mean, spiteful, or harmful to me. He has always shown me nothing but love but for years the enemy had me drinking that poison focusing on what I didn't have over what I did.

It honestly wasn't until recently, maybe around 2018, that I began to verbalize to others as well as myself during the process that certain things happening to me just were not my problem yet an indicator to someone else's deep seated issues. I needed to be firmer on my values and not discount myself because of other's shortcomings. I found myself frequently saying "I'm not taking that on. That's not my problem!" That toxic mindset and behavior of internalizing external or other people's issues was smothering me from living fully in my worth and value as one of God's daughters. It was blinding me from seeing myself for who I truly was, and it was time for it to go!

DIVORCE DECLARATION

I AM NO LONGER A DISCOUNTED DOLL!

I am divorced from this toxic mindset and disassociate myself with any past unworthy behavior. I curse any memories of this behavior with intentions to taunt or paralyze me in my heart, mind, body, and soul and speak everything good over my life –value and priceless worth!

STATEMENT OF IDENTITY

I AM A WOMAN OF GODLY STANDARDS, *worth and value! I will not compromise my worth to make others comfortable but will allow my love to be an example to all who I encounter even those who do wrong by me. I will speak my truth and no longer hold my truth and others truth in shame because I realize it is the truth that frees us. Other's perception and treatment of me does not define me but I am defined through the redemption I have received from Jesus Christ. I am His and I am handpicked for His purpose.*

The Compromised Companion - Settling For Less

Companionship is a basic human need yet can be complex when you take into account that every human's perspective and personal acceptance of connection is different. That aspect makes companionship a little more challenging but when it is found it is worth it. We all desire the fundamental aspects of companionship like connection, attention, and love. We desire our companion to be someone we share mutual love, respect, trust, and commitment with. A companion is your best friend – the one you can bare your soul to without judgment, share your quirky, weird, or deep side to, it is someone who loves you for who you are –flaws and all.

When I speak of companion in this chapter I'm referencing that of an intimate relationship, a soul mate, or the one you're willing to spend forever with. This pristine view of how relationships should feel and look through lens of companionship fills me with every good, warm, and uplifting feeling. Yet what I didn't know is my carelessness of allowing wrong choices and mistakes rule my mind and spirit began to taint my pure view.

When I wasn't getting what I thought I deserved quick enough, I began to grow weary in what seemed like a never-ending winter season. Malinda Thomas, author of The Deborah Anointing, defined winter as such, "Your spiritual winter can seem like a time of darkness, as if your life is unfruitful, and you may assume your dreams are dying. But during winter there is no fruit bearing. It is a time when God kills everything in your life that will affect the harvest of the next season in your life."

My winter seasons were gruesome and seemed to have

no end. My love life especially felt like a drought. My desire to be loved and in a relationship seemed so far from reality because I wasn't even being asked on dates. It seemed as if no one was even interested in me or the ones that were, I wasn't, because I knew they wouldn't be a good fit for me. Because truth be told, the many winters have drawn me closer to God and my purpose. As He stripped away dead things, He'd plant new ideas and character traits in me making me grow and glow. Yet even with all the growing and glowing, aspiring and accomplishing within His purpose for me, that area of companionship somehow still remained cold and uncomfortable.

My growth and maturity equipped me to know what I wanted (which is why I was easily able to discern whether someone was for me or just intrigued by His light in me). I wanted a man of God, just as bold and crazy in love with the Lord as I was. I wanted someone I could build with, nothing less than a power couple in every sector of life- spiritual, business, etc. I wanted someone who desired to live life to the fullest like myself and create legacy for our family. A businessman who is a visionary so we could chase our wildest dreams together. Someone who was not intimidated by my shine but supportive and motivated by it. Someone who would be excited yet patient in learning love & marriage with me.

I live my life wanting to be an example and inspiration to others. I wanted my relationship to do the same. But what I wanted seemed to not exist. I even grew resentful toward God. I was confident He heard my prayers and attended to my needs and desires; yet it felt like His ears were closed in my strong desire for a husband. I felt teased by the men who made it past first base and piqued my interest to only leave the entire game with no explanation or even to be with someone else. This my friends, almost seemed like a cycle to me, it has been going on for a solid 12 years of feeling like the coldest and longest winter ever. I was involved with what I believed real potential a few times over those years but that cycle seemed to repeat –to give yourself and begin to open up and build with someone to only have them leave you to be with someone else. And the crazy thing was that every man that left would always try to come back confessing how the grass wasn't greener on the other side. It shattered my heart each time, bringing me into Discounted Doll moments. I thought, "I must not be enough, something is wrong with me."

A couple years ago I got tired of waiting on God. Tired of not feeling loved while seeing everyone around me have someone special. I was tired of everyone asking when I was going to have children. When I would reply, "When my husband comes," they'd say, "Well he better hurry up, you're not getting any younger!" or "You know childbirth is harder the older you get, be careful!" It was annoying, disappointing, and infuriating at times. I was tired of being overlooked. I wondered if there was a sticker on my head that said "Stay Away."

I was exhausted from "uplifting" remarks about "men being intimidated by me," or "You work too much to be found." I was sick and tired of believing and hoping that I'd never experience what my heart wanted. The warm feelings and thoughts about a companion were growing cold. Some other toxic behaviors had their way with me in that long dark space. "I Deserve" showed up. I felt like I was wasting my youthful baby making years, waiting on a man I was beginning to believe would never come.

"I Deserve" began to empower me in a negative direction telling me to grab hold of "The Rebel" and get what you want and deserve. I began to feel sorry for myself, the humiliation of never being chosen raged in my mind, and the compromised companion was born. I began to convince myself it was okay to settle for something less than what I wanted. At least I was getting attention/some needs met. The Rebel in me was firing up and ready to eliminate any barriers and get what I wanted at any cost, even if it hurt others along that way. During this time, I entered into one of the most toxic relationships of my life.

I had every reason not to be with this person, but I was in a place of being willing to compromise my personal standards as well as my standards as a Daughter of the King for my personal satisfaction. I compromised my purity, dignity, loyalty, worth, hope, credibility, spiritual and personal growth, friendships for this secret of a man I held so close to my heart. He spoke the language the compromised and settling companion in me would thrive on because my expectations were shot out- COMPLETELY!

Mentally I justified my relationship with him solely based on my own needs even though he couldn't even fully meet them. I would make excuses for his lack of commitment like "well I'm focused on building my business. I don't have time for a relationship!" or "I don't need that attention! Just give me what I want, when I want it!" I was in a low and lying place. Truth is, I need attention, actually a lot of attention but here I was compromising my need for a temporal fix. I did need to focus on my business but deep in my heart I wanted someone to navigate that with me. Someone to talk to about my fresh ideas and to give me feedback and insight.

My spiritual life took a huge hit during this time. Attending church wasn't the problem, it was my personal relationship that was at risk. I lost, well betrayed, my closest friend. I couldn't hear God as clearly as before; I began to have issues with my non-profit and business. Somehow the woman who wanted her relationship to be an example and inspiration to others, found herself in a relationship that she kept a secret from her family and friends. I was too ashamed and embarrassed to share because I know I was worth more. Being the compromised companion was just as exhausting as waiting on my desires from God; my spiritual life was spiraling out of control. I knew I had to divorce this toxic mindset, and relationship. I had a prodigal son moment.

Honestly, that was my main focus—to return to my dearest and closest friend, God. I still had little hope of getting the man I desired, all these years of being run down on by others and myself, if I could just be in right standing with God—I was Good!! One day at one of our prayer retreats our leader pulled two chairs up and told me to sit down next to my husband. In my head, I let out a huge sigh of irritation and an eye roll because my faith for a husband was deteriorating and causing me to question God, but I was obedient.

I sat in the chair and began to pray for him. God showed me some amazing things about him, confirming a lot of what I shared earlier. He shared my role in covering Him constantly in prayer and love as he had endured some family pain and issues that weighed on him heavily and he carries a lot of the pain in silence. He told me how I would be a refuge for him and showed him how to love and be loved properly. That scared and excited me at the same time. I began to hope again and shift my mind from compromised companion to the Called Companion – realizing it was more than just a marriage, but a calling I have for this man out there somewhere. When we connect, I'd be part of his healing.

DIVORCE DECLARATION

I AM NO LONGER A COMPROMISED COMPANION!

I am divorced from this toxic mindset and disassociate myself with any past settling and compromising behavior. I curse any memories of this behavior with intentions to taunt or paralyze me in my heart, mind, body, and soul and speak everything good over my life - value and priceless worth!

STATEMENT OF IDENTITY

I AM GOD'S DAUGHTER. HIS FAVORITE. HANDPICKED BY HIM.

I am no longer weak in waiting yet focused on His purpose and serving Him with patience. I trust that His timing is perfect like He is and understand as His friend He would never want me to settle for something less than what He has prepared for me. He will approve the right man to have me. I rest my future marriage in Him.

The Broken Savage- Numbing The Pain

Numbing the pain is temporal. I recall a time where I stood in as the support person for my sister as she underwent surgery and the pain teams reviewed the benefits as well as potential dangers of her pain management options. I stayed close to my sister as she sat with the critical decision making at hand along with processing the potential pain of the "numbing options". I asked them questions about how long these options will hold the pain back. They told me it varies, from 12-30 hours. No matter how you looked at it, the options only temporarily numbed the pain. She would soon be met with the reality of the pain and be left to manage it herself.

The Broken Savage mindset is one that is full of behaviors that only numb a deeper pain and sometimes cause you to form addiction to a temporary "soother" so you don't have to face the pain.

The reality of the matter is numbing the pain doesn't take it away. It still exists; it still has life because we're choosing to silence it rather than evict or kill it. There was a point in my life that I called savage season where numbing and pain management were at an all-time high. Let's talk about it.

It's one thing when you're going through a rough time and you turn to your worship music, prayer, girl time, or family to get through. It's a whole other story when you find yourself turning to a bottle, sex, and a "carefree" lifestyle to get you through. I remember the particular season when I declared to my friends I was going into Savage mode. They didn't encourage it, yet they knew I was fresh off of bad heartbreak and quite sick and tired of being the nice person who was always done wrong in the end. I gave this "situationship" a good 2-3 years of my time and energy for this man to put me on a pedestal (I deserve mindset) that I didn't ask for and decide it'd be better to try a relationship with someone else because I was just "too special."

When I tell y'all I was crushed! The intense range of emotions made me feel crazy. Sadness and confusion turned to anger and bitterness, then to resentment and rage toward men. My Christian standards were on a steep decline. My mind wandered – Is there really someone out there that can treat me the way "I deserve", someone I can exchange love with... If I'm so "Handpicked," why do I get treated so poorly... I'm preserving and saving myself for what?!

I recall finding some functionality in life, spending a Friday night out in the city, only to run into this man and his new woman. He wanted to still be friends but it was all too much for me. I decided I'd just hit Savage mode. Webster defines savage as *a brutal or vicious person- fierce, violent and uncontrolled.*

I had planned to be just that since it seemed like being nice, loving, patient, enduring, and hopeful got me nowhere. Savage mode meant I would turn to a "I need to do me" attitude which meant that whatever benefited or pleased me was what I would be found doing. I felt like I reconnected with my young, wild college years, where maturity and doing the right thing all the time wasn't expected and even if it was... I wasn't doing it. I was in a place of challenging almost every standard I built trying to find a version of me that didn't require great responsibility or expectation. I would soon find out that the consequences of employing that savage version of myself would cost me more pain in the long run.

If I had dealt with the pain initially, then maybe I wouldn't have to deal with the deep-seated pain along with the shame and scarring the numbing factors caused. Not requiring standards out of men, only looking for them to fill time and physical needs was a damaging numbing factor. Filling my nights and weekends with being out and about, "living the life" while trying to still hold onto a bit of my faith was a numbing factor that confused both myself and others. I was broken! After awhile, the weeping, sadness, resentment, bitterness, and discontentment resurfaced again, either the numbing had worn off, or I needed to find something new to numb my pain.

Thank God I was wise enough to know this savage mode was unhealthy for me and I was desperately missing the peace and assurance felt while in and under God's care. But before I could just turn savage mode off, God made me look deeper into myself. This particular savage season was caused by a heartbreak, yet as we've learned through this book, it's imperative we find the root, and we know many times the root isn't what we see in plain sight. I began to scan my life for past "savage mode" moments. When did this start? When did I start numbing my pain? I traced pain all the way back to childhood, but I couldn't identify any distinct numbing factors.

So, I moved along my search and came to a time that hit pretty hard for me. It was a time where I was numb physically, mentally, emotionally, and even spiritually...it was when I met GRIEF for the first time!!! In 2012 my sister blessed this world with 3 triplets. They were born at 26 weeks and are true miracle babies. We spent the first 9 months of their lives in the hospital, and we were by their side every step of the way – through surgeries, respiratory failures, meningitis, multiple hospitals and rehab centers, and way too many close calls.

Quite like myself, my nieces didn't have their father in their lives, so I vowed to be the best support to them and my sister as possible. These 3 little girls changed my life completely, and their state of need rustled up a strength, endurance, tenacity, and love in me that I didn't know existed. Their suffering and survival matured me, stretched my faith, and enhanced my perspective on life. My girls suffered long and hard during their time in the hospital, but my family and I relied heavily on God throughout the entire time. Every hospital we'd land at would grow accustomed to finding us praying, playing worship music, and speaking our faith in the face of the most adverse declarations from "the experts."

Having that faith was both challenging yet comforting but that shifted for me Feb 2013 when our precious Nia suddenly passed away. I can flash back to that moment like it was yesterday from receiving the call to rush to the hospital from my sister, to holding her dr. up in my arms after she told me she was gone, to marching to her room with all faith for a Lazarus miracl, to hearing God tell me she's safe and resting now. That was the most painful day of my life which turned into the most painful season of my life. I've buried many friends and loved ones prior to Nia, I thought I knew what grief was, but I was experiencing it on a crippling level. I couldn't understand why or what happened! I blamed the hospital for it because she was fine until they took her in for observation!

I questioned God, "How could you take her after we've been standing in such great faith for so long?" I was crushed because I couldn't keep my promises of sleepovers and shopping days to my little girl. She would never get to see her sisters, let alone play and grow with them. I'm known as a talker and not usually found without words often, yet during this season I had no words... my prayers were of a few words "God help me" and full of uncertainty.

My entire being was numb like the pain and disbelief was so great I didn't feel anything. The stress of the grief and still dealing with two other babies in the hospital along with other family matters, I excused myself for a drink from time to time when I would escape for a girl's night with friends. An innocent dinner at the winery wasn't so innocent as that bottle I took home became my escape. I would spend many nights crying or with my mind running a mile per minute feeding off the grief, anxiety, and emptiness. The nights got longer where I couldn't sleep, and I began to drink every night so I could. It wasn't hard liquor; it was only wine, but the root of the issue was is it was numbing the pain and providing me with temporal relief.

Many would say well it wasn't hard liquor or drugs, you didn't turn into an alcoholic, you're blowing this out of proportion, but addiction wasn't my issue. My issue was my faith was greater in the wine, a temporary fix, than in God, the permanent solution. I remember one night saying to God, "You must give me something to get through this or I'm not going to make it."

The next morning while riding to work, a song, "Not For A Moment" by Meridith Andrews, dropped in my heart. I played it on repeat for months. It was my hope, faith, and voice. For a long time, I just remember being numb. It spoke directly to the looming depression over me, feeling lost, going through the motions of life, far from any sense of purpose and the creator of my purpose. Yet, it assured me that after all God is still God and there is not a moment in time He will turn His back on me.

These lyrics carried me to a breakthrough. I was reconnected with the purpose stirring in me in spite of the grief and loss and my call to complete it.

DIVORCE DECLARATION

I AM NO LONGER A BROKEN SAVAGE

I am divorced from this toxic mindset and disassociate myself with any past reckless, savage behavior. I curse any memories of this behavior with intentions to taunt or paralyze me in my heart, mind, body, and soul and speak everything good over my life – value and priceless worth!

STATEMENT OF IDENTITY

I NO LONGER NEED TO DO ME, I ONLY NEED TO DO THE WORK OF MY FATHER

" So Jesus explained, "I tell you the truth, the Son can do nothing by himself. He does only what he sees the Father doing. Whatever the Father does, the Son also does. For the Father loves the Son and shows him everything he is doing. In fact, the Father will show him how to do even greater works than healing this man. Then you will truly be astonished"
John 5: 19-20 NLT

And indeed you are showing me the greater works and I am astonished by how you have transformed my life. My plans were emotionally driven and destructive but yours have rescued me from my own plans and given me a life greater than I can imagine as your daughter and disciple.

PERMISSION TO PAUSE

What feelings do you have connected to divorce? Is it scary, sensitive, unknown?

_____

_____

_____

_____

What are some deep dark parts of you that you need to be cleansed and heal? Are you ready to be raw and real with yourself and God? (PS God knows anyway)

_____

_____

_____

_____

_____

How are you feeling about facing your own toxic mindsets?
It can be overwhelming. Take your time. It took me months to process each of these toxic mindsets because they were HEAVY. I had to really look in the mirror and see myself and choose healing, and that my friend requires time.

_____

_____

_____

_____

_____

_____

_____

_____

NO JUDGEMENT ZONE

Dismantling Toxic Mindsets
W O R K S H E E T

This worksheet will help you to identify the toxic mindsets, explore how it has attached itself to you, learn how it has shown up in your life, and make a plan of action to fight the mindset and create a healthy one.

PART 1: The Story
Identify the toxic mindset and what happened to cause it.

_____

_____

_____

_____

_____

_____

_____

PART 2: Divorce Declaration
This is where you declare "I am not (insert toxic mindset)" and proceed to announce what you will curse, disassociate, and divorce.

_____

_____

_____

_____

_____

_____

_____

_____

PART 3: Statement Of Identity
This is where you proclaim who you are in Christ now that you have divorced this mindset

_____

_____

_____

_____

_____

_____

_____

_____

_____

Dismantling Toxic Mindsets
W O R K S H E E T

This worksheet will help you to identify the toxic mindsets, explore how it has attached itself to you, learn how it has shown up in your life, and make a plan of action to fight the mindset and create a healthy one.

PART 1: The Story
Identify the toxic mindset and what happened to cause it.

_____
_____
_____
_____
_____
_____
_____
_____

PART 2: Divorce Declaration
This is where you declare "I am not (insert toxic mindset)" and proceed to announce what you will curse, disassociate, and divorce.

_____
_____
_____
_____
_____
_____
_____
_____

PART 3: Statement Of Identity
This is where you proclaim who you are in Christ now that you have divorced this mindset

_____
_____
_____
_____
_____
_____
_____
_____

Dear Healing

Thank you for the courage to
tell my story from the lens of
purpose not pain. My
vulnerability has met
The Savior's redemption,
and I am thankful!

5

I CHOSE HEALING

I'm so glad that I chose healing over hurt. That decision produced purpose and peace in my life opposed to pain and pity. When we choose our hurt over healing, we continually hurt those around us. Not only are we blinded by the hurt that is within us, we're also blinded by the hurt that we inflict on others and how it can affect our legacy. Because whatever is happening in the darkness even if it's in the dark places within you will be brought to the light (Luke 8:17). At some point in time that hurt, unresolved resentment, and pain that is brewing will manifest, and will be visible for all to see, not just the ones that you are inflicting hurt on. Unresolved hurt and pain will have you accusing others of things that have nothing to do with them but everything to do with the root of your own pain and hurt.

I've had friendships, associations, and even relationships destroyed because of people's perception of me through their eyes of pain. Unaddressed pain causes one to look and see things through their blurred perspective — the images they see are distorted based off of their experiences of hurt, pain, neglect, abandonment, mistreatment and resentment. These individuals typically assume the worst, accuse without sound reasoning, display red flags as those who can't be trusted simply because they are ruled by their pain.

I want to share a few life lessons I've learned navigating healing whether it be from intimate relationships, friendships, family and even with God.

GOD HAS *Healed Me*

FROM A BRUISED AND BROKEN HEART

Lessons From My Healing Journey:

1. A man must prove through words and actions his ability to handle a woman.
2. All parties should be on the same page, not just you and God
3. You can't pick apart others and not look at yourself. This is why Divorcing Me is necessary in your process
4. Timing is everything, heed it
5. Forgiving yourself is a requirement
6. Patience is a strong, subtle gift necessary for faith activation
7. Don't give away the best parts of you too soon
8. Sex makes everything hazy. Build and grow with God and without it until " I Do"
9. Trust the signs! Do not ignore the red flags in any relationship
10. Dependence on God is your lifeline
11. Be willing to shed the weight over just a glimpse of your destiny
12. I am a beautiful, strong and loving reflection of God – never trading my crown even if mud is thrown at it
13. I am healing and I am a healer
14. Beware of too many voices during a time of exploring and decision making
15. Holding emotions in does you no good
16. It stings worse when you haven't let go of old stuff
17. Being self aware is a great tool for sustaining healing
18. Producing our of your pain can birth mess but producing out of your healing brings great purpose

19. Consecration and Communion are power players when you desire to die to your flesh
20. Lean into God during challenges! Don't run away from the Repairer
21. Healing alone is practically impossible. Build your tribe. If they can see you through the hurt, they should be able to see you through the healing
22. Let go of your "Should have beens" to receive your "Shall be"
23. Everything is a choice. Choose healing over hurt, forgiveness over resentment, progress over complacency. Choose the chosen way of God.
24. The Holy Spirit affirms and empowers who I am, what I need, and my desires
25. React to God's warnings, don't just hear them
26. Never let your personal desires grow stronger than your obedience to the Lord
27. Don't limit who or what God can use to speak to you
28. Truth hurts, yet it also makes you free

I can now say though it took some time, tears, and acceptance... I'm better, I made it through my process, but most importantly I allowed it to strengthen my relationship with God! I believe this is your portion too.

I want to close with the 5 B's of Healing. We've shaken up and uprooted some things through the lens of faith, realizing that identifying our bruises, pain, trauma, loss, can lead us on a journey that will set us free from it. Be means to: *exist, live, to occupy a place, position, or situation.* I want you to BE in God. He is a position of permanency, a place where you feel safe to rest or settle.

"Be's of Healing"

1. Be raw and real

2. Be brave and bold

3. Be open and humble

4. Be committed to the process

5. Be in God's face and presence

If you can find yourself being all of these things as you represent Christ, you will experience your connection to God, yourself, and others transform before you very eyes. This state of transparency, self-awareness, soundness of faith will keep you continuously blessed, free from people who aren't for you, and close to the heart and ear of God, concerning you and His kingdom.

From Bruised to Blessed

Beauty, YOU MADE IT! What you endured has only prepared you for the next level. Pain and trauma fight to define us and wreck our identity. That is why this healing work is so important, not only to your freedom but your growth and purpose. Healing is the surgery, but sustainability is the physical therapy. Now that the bruises are fading, it's time for strength training, where you become comfortable in your newness and obtain daily discipline of relying on God as your source. You aren't just surviving the trauma anymore; you are building the core strength required to carry the blessings coming in the next phase.

Lesson #21 reminded us of the importance of a tribe as you're healing. Within the next 24 hours, reach out to one person you trust—a mentor, a friend, or a sister in Christ. Share one specific area where you have found freedom in this book. Healing is sealed when it is shared.

Volume 2 of the Healing Journey is focused on how blessed you truly are! To survive what you have been through, to be forgiven for what you've done, and be redeemed and restored with an everlasting plan and purpose for your life, on Earth and in Heaven. It's time that you reconnect with your dreams and God's plan for you by redefining your identity, worth and value in Christ. It's graduation time!

YOU MADE IT

The Courage To Heal

C H E C K L I S T

This worksheet serves as an essential self-assessment tool for participants concluding Part 1 of The Healing Journey program. It will guide you through five specific and actionable "Checks" to verify your progress and solidify their healing.

Identity Check

Can you list three truths about who God says you are?

_____

_____

_____

Boundary Check

Have you removed or reassessed the "places and things" that hinder your standard?

☐ Yes   ☐ No   ☐ I'm Working On It

_____

_____

Voice Check

Have you silenced the "bass" in the voice of your past?

☐ Yes   ☐ No   ☐ I'm Working On It

_____

_____

_____

Foundation Check

Is your relationship with the Father reciprocal rather than transactional?

☐ Reciprocal   ☐ Transactional

_____

_____

Community Check

Have you identified at least 2 people for your "healing tribe"?

☐ Yes   ☐ No   ☐ I'm Working On It

1._____

2._____

Dear Healing

This journey has not been an easy
one. It was full of tears, forgiveness,
accountability, and facing things
I wanted to forget, but I survived.
I want to see what more
is in store for me!
Thank you for leading me!

This is your last permission to pause. Sis you've made it through the bruised phase to healing. How are you feeling?

_____

_____

_____

_____

_____

_____

_____

_____

_____

What lessons have you learned?

_____

_____

_____

_____

_____

_____

_____

_____

_____

_____

Letter of Release
W O R K S H E E T

During my process, I had to write several letters to empty my soul and heart of various situations. I also had to write a letter to myself to welcome forgiveness and promise growth and blessings because I was surely living in both despite what I'd been through.

This worksheets are for you to write your necessary letters. You may be led to send them to the individual, or you may just need to release it, but either way, the Holy Spirit will guide you. Psalm 34:14

_____
_____
_____
_____
_____
_____
_____
_____
_____
_____
_____
_____
_____
_____
_____
_____
_____
_____
_____
_____
_____
_____
_____
_____
_____
_____

Letter of Release
WORKSHEET

During my process, I had to write several letters to empty my soul and heart of various situations. I also had to write a letter to myself to welcome forgiveness and promise growth and blessings because I was surely living in both despite what I'd been through.

This worksheets are for you to write your necessary letters. You may be led to send them to the individual, or you may just need to release it, but either way, the Holy Spirit will guide you. Psalm 34:14

_____

_____

_____

_____

_____

_____

_____

_____

_____

_____

_____

_____

_____

_____

_____

_____

_____

_____

_____

_____

_____

_____

_____

_____

_____

_____

_____

_____

_____

Letter of Release
WORKSHEET

During my process, I had to write several letters to empty my soul and heart of various situations. I also had to write a letter to myself to welcome forgiveness and promise growth and blessings because I was surely living in both despite what I'd been through.

This worksheets are for you to write your necessary letters. You may be led to send them to the individual, or you may just need to release it, but either way, the Holy Spirit will guide you. Psalm 34:14

_____

_____

_____

_____

_____

_____

_____

_____

_____

_____

_____

_____

_____

_____

_____

_____

_____

_____

_____

_____

_____

_____

_____

_____

_____

Connect with Soleil: www.iamhandpicked.org
Facebook & Instagram: @SoleilMeade